To Linda,

This book is dedicated to those who stood by me through difficult times, and have continued to support me. And you are one of those.

Thank You.

With Love,

Helen Jones

xxx

from Laura xxxx

I am a Real Person

Helen Jones

authorHOUSE®

AuthorHouse™ UK
1663 Liberty Drive
Bloomington, IN 47403 USA
www.authorhouse.co.uk
Phone: UK TFN: 0800 0148641 (Toll Free inside the UK)
UK Local: 02036 956322 (+44 20 3695 6322 from outside the UK)

© 2021 Helen Jones. All rights reserved.

No part of this book may be reproduced, stored in a retrieval system, or transmitted by any means without the written permission of the author.

Published by AuthorHouse 03/10/2021

ISBN: 978-1-6655-8147-9 (sc)
ISBN: 978-1-6655-8698-6 (e)

Library of Congress Control Number: 2021904581

Print information available on the last page.

This book is printed on acid-free paper.

Because of the dynamic nature of the Internet, any web addresses or links contained in this book may have changed since publication and may no longer be valid. The views expressed in this work are solely those of the author and do not necessarily reflect the views of the publisher, and the publisher hereby disclaims any responsibility for them.

CONTENTS

Chapter 1	The Beginning of the End	1
Chapter 2	Childhood	12
Chapter 3	Teenage Angst	21
Chapter 4	Bicycles and Scooters	31
Chapter 5	First Love	37
Chapter 6	A Working Girl	41
Chapter 7	First Boyfriend	48
Chapter 8	Hannah Gets Married	52
Chapter 9	Independence	57
Chapter 10	Meeting Jim	62
Chapter 11	Courtship and Marriage	67
Chapter 12	Peterborough	75
Chapter 13	Parents Again	80
Chapter 14	Housed at Last	86
Chapter 15	On the Buses	94
Chapter 16	Cleaner of the Year	101
Chapter 17	Camping	106
Chapter 18	Jonno	114
Chapter 19	Another New Start	122
Chapter 20	Out of London	135
Chapter 21	Life Goes On	140
Chapter 22	A Proper Council House	144
Chapter 23	Old Friends	149
Chapter 24	The Struggle Is Real	155
Chapter 25	The Joy of Having Teenagers	162
Chapter 26	New Neighbours	169
Chapter 27	A Moment of Realisation	174

Chapter 28 Loss and New Life	178
Chapter 29 From Bad to Worse	186
Chapter 30 Countdown	192
Chapter 31 Escape!	199
Chapter 32 The Refuge	205
Chapter 33 The Next Chapter	213

Behind Closed Doors

A guarded secret
Clothed in shame,
Abused and battered.
No one knows.
He loved her once—
So why? She cries.
Violence, jealousy, threats,
And worse.
Don't give up.
Your life is precious,
A gift from God.
He knows, sees all,
And loves you still.
He wraps his arms around you.
There is a future yet.
—Helen Jones

CHAPTER 1

The Beginning of the End

THE DIFFICULTIES AND PRESSURES IN my life were mounting to an unbearable pitch. To be dead was preferable. But there were the children to think of, especially the little ones. I didn't think at the time that they knew or understood what was happening to me. They just thought Mummy and Daddy went for a walk by the river or for a drink in the Jolly Farmers in the evenings. If it had been as simple as that, we could've taken them along for a family evening together. The river and surrounding countryside were lovely at any time of the year, and the pub had a big garden with a colourful climbing frame and swings, which the children would've loved. But it wasn't as simple as that.

My older children were growing up and leaving home. Only Mark was left. He was 17 and out of school, with no work prospects in view. My husband was also unemployed, although this was usual for him. He was always either unemployed or supposedly ill. Because of this, money was very tight, and what little we had, my husband would squander on all sorts of frivolities, as well as his cigarettes and alcohol. I had to do my shopping with the weekly family allowance (a small government payment awarded to families with children, now known as child benefit), while various bills went unpaid. So there were constant knocks on the door from debt collectors and bailiffs.

Finally, in desperation, I got a job. Desperate for the money to feed my family, and desperate to get away from the misery at home. The first job that came my way was factory work. I didn't have the confidence to do anything more academic, so I took the job. I worked full-time, leaving home at seven in the morning for an eight o'clock start. I found the work exhausting, especially having to come home at five o'clock to start on the housework, washing, and so on. I did often get my dinner cooked though as my husband, Jim, enjoyed cooking.

It was a new and fascinating experience working in the factory. The work itself was incredibly boring and most of the workers were extremely coarse, but they were certainly a happy crowd. For all their moaning and groaning about the work and the chargehands, they seemed to enjoy themselves and have a good laugh.

I worked with Carla, a very pretty, cheeky, world-wise 16-year-old. She had beautiful, long red curls and was especially popular with the lads. Carla and I got on well together, despite our being complete opposites and the obvious age difference.

While at the factory, I formed a friendship with a young lad named Marty, who was about the same age as my eldest daughter. He was a very conscientious worker. And one day a week, he attended college. For two or three evenings each week, he taught judo to youngsters at a local club, being a black belt himself and proud of it. He was quite sporty and liked to keep fit, usually coming to work on his racing bike. But he didn't fit into the usual mould of factory boys, so unfortunately he was prime material for leg pulling.

I must admit I did join in with the teasing at first, even to the extent of writing a poem! This started off with teasing about his judo interest, with the lads calling him the Karate Kid, which he hated. Carla and I thought we'd go one better. We had our own private joke that he wasn't a martial arts expert at all. Just between the two of us, we joked that perhaps he was really a secret trainspotter or perhaps into fishing or even a ping-pong expert. Maybe he was even into marbles or kite flying! We didn't mean to offend him, but every time we looked at Marty, we collapsed in giggles until eventually he wanted to know what we were laughing at. We wouldn't tell him at first, but that evening, I wrote the aforementioned poem. It went as follows:

> To Marty, champion of martial arts,
> Could it be kung fu?

I AM A REAL PERSON

> Could it be karate?
> Or maybe jujitsu?
> We think you're bluffing, Marty.
> We've sussed you out at last,
> So all this judo rubbish
> Will now be in the past.
> We think that you're out fishing
> When you're not at work,
> But it doesn't sound too manly.
> In fact, a fisherman's a jerk!
> Or table tennis, Marty—
> Is that your little game?
> Or bird watching? That's it—
> Something feeble just the same.
> So don't try bluffing anymore.
> Your game is up and so—
> No more judo rubbish, please,
> 'Cause, Marty, now we *know*—
> You're the underwater tiddlywinks champion of Orpington!

When I showed the Carla the next morning, we both fell about laughing. For the rest of that day, we couldn't look at Marty without collapsing in hysterics. By the end of the day, the poor boy was completely paranoid. He kept asking us what was so funny, and I said he'd know at the end of the day. During our lunch break, I wrote out a neat copy of the poem for him so that he could finally have a good laugh with us.

When it was time to go home, I found Marty waiting for me and handed him the carefully folded paper. Before even opening it, he flushed a deep pink so I left hurriedly, thinking it might be best to share the joke the following day.

On the way home, Carla and I got the giggles again. She said that maybe Marty had thought I was giving him a love letter! No wonder he'd blushed.

But there was to be no sharing of the joke with Marty. He came to work the next day with a face so long he could've tripped over it. *Surely not a reaction to the poem?* we thought. I tried a hello and a smile, but he looked the other way each time. We couldn't believe that something so trivial could have upset him so much. As the day wore on, Marty looked more and more unhappy, and I began to feel more and more guilty. In the end, I felt compelled to go over to him and ask him what was wrong.

"No, I didn't think it was funny," he told me. "It was just about the last straw."

I assured him that we hadn't meant any offence. He should have been pleased because if we hadn't thought of him as a friend, we would never have bothered writing a poem for him. He just grumbled quietly so I went back to my own workbench and carried on packing boxes. Carla said if he couldn't take a joke, he wasn't worth bothering with. But when I saw him glance across at me, I smiled back, hoping to reassure him that I didn't feel badly towards him. At the end of the day's work, he crossed the factory floor and stood silently beside me. I said again that I was sorry to have offended him. I think he then realised that I wasn't any sort of a threat, and he started to talk to me at last.

Over the following weeks, we got to know each other well, and I learned that Marty had a lot of problems weighing heavily on him. He seemed to need someone to confide in, and gradually that someone became me. The others, Carla included, couldn't be bothered with him anymore, so the two of us would often spend our lunch breaks together, either just chatting or with me riding his bike round the factory car park. I remember one time I was going rather fast and lost control. I almost careered into our boss as he drove round the corner from the executives' car park. The others, having their lunch, saw the whole incident through the canteen window and teased us mercilessly for several weeks afterwards.

Another day, I brought in a collection of photographs to show him. They were pictures that my husband had taken when he had been a marshal at Brands Hatch a few years earlier. Motor racing was something that Marty was very interested in.

We gradually became good friends, and sometimes I would tease him gently, at the same time remembering his sensitivity.

For a long time, he continued to confide in me. He told me his mother had abandoned him at an early age. Although he had an older sister and a father somewhere on the scene, he lived with and had been brought up by his paternal grandmother. I thought that perhaps he was looking for a mother figure. I didn't mind. I was growing very fond of him.

Unfortunately, others in the factory, our chargehand included, could see this. Unknown to me, they began to taunt Marty about his "friendship" with me, an older woman.

I first knew something was wrong when he suddenly withdrew from me. I tried to catch his eye across the factory floor as we always had done, but he'd immediately look away. I couldn't understand what the matter was. When I approached him directly, he refused to talk to me. I was so upset that after a few days of this, I asked Carla if she knew why he was avoiding me. That was when I finally found out about the gossip and the teasing. I felt very hurt for Marty, knowing how sensitive he could be. He still avoided eye contact with me, while at other times, I could sense him looking across at me with his sad eyes.

At work, this really bothered me. But worse still, I could not put it out of my mind, even when I got home. He was permanently in my thoughts. Eventually, I realised I was not only upset for him but also desperately upset for myself. The factory gossips had been right. We were becoming too close, and everybody had been aware of it except for me. How could I have been so blind?

In the end, I had to admit the truth to myself. I loved that boy. I loved him for his honesty, his sensitivity, and his dedication to everything that he did.

The times that we had spent together at the factory had been happy times, and we'd been so comfortable together. I really missed him now. At home, in the privacy of my bath, I'd cry so much, then when I'd finished bathing, I'd scrub my face clean and come out of the bathroom all rosy and pink, and no one would guess how I'd really spent the last half hour.

I felt bad though. I felt as if I'd betrayed my husband and family. I really believed in the sanctity of marriage and hated myself for having feelings for someone else. Had I been happy at home, and felt loved and cared for, I feel almost certain that this situation would not have come about. As well as having a guilty conscience over it all, I also felt frightened. Frightened to think of what the consequences could be if these feelings were followed up. It shocked me to think I was capable of being unfaithful to my husband—and with a boy the same age as my own daughter. I hated myself for it, especially as the truth of it was all we'd ever done was talk.

During these months at the factory, the problems with my husband continued. The night-times got worse, and I was afraid to go to sleep. I'd lie rigid for hours on my side of the bed, listening to his breathing. I used to think that if his breathing stopped, I could sleep peacefully and pretend to know nothing about it until the morning. The next best thing was when his breathing grew heavier and I knew he was asleep. Only then could I relax a little, though even then, he rarely slept the night through.

Often in the early hours of the morning, he'd wake up and demand that I fetch him a drink of water. At first, I used to ignore him and pretend to be still asleep, but he'd thrash about in the bed and shout at me until it was obvious that I wasn't, and if I protested, his set answer was always "If I can't sleep, I don't see why you should." Once I'd supplied him with his drink, he'd start on a marathon sexual performance of one perverted kind or another, which would mean between two to four hours of no sleep and excessive pain. In the end, I figured that the sooner I got up and got him his water, the sooner the whole awful business was over for another night.

I always tried to keep quiet through everything so not to disturb or frighten the younger children. But sometimes it was just too terrifying. He'd put his huge hands around my throat and squeeze while performing his sexual act on me, or other times he'd just push a pillow over my face. Somehow I always seemed to find superhuman strength to fight my way out, and then if I could get away, I'd run into one of the older children's bedrooms for sanctuary.

Those eldest three of my children all knew that things were badly wrong, and they hated their father. Not only had they witnessed some of the violence shown to me, but he'd also failed to be a good father to them, breaking promises and failing to provide them with their basic needs.

My eldest son was another main target of his father's bullying and his fists. Although they were afraid of their father, most of the time, we all played at "happy families" and pretended, even to ourselves, that nothing was wrong. Their three younger siblings, I thought, were completely unaware of any difficulties, and I made every effort to protect them from it.

But now, our eldest two children had left home. Melissa lived with her partner, Tom, and their beautiful little girl, Eliza, in a neighbouring town, and my son, Scott, lived nearby in foster care. He'd been there since his early teens to escape his father's brutality. Mark still lived at home. He was a mild-tempered boy who really hated the obvious unhappiness and discord at home and had vowed to move out as soon as he was 18, at which age he would be eligible for social security benefits if still unemployed so in a position to support himself.

I dreaded the thought of Mark leaving home. It would mean there was no older son or daughter to run to in the night. The three youngest were too little to involve in this or to help in any way.

Since very early on in our marriage, my husband had nurtured an obsession with me going to the toilet. He wanted to watch me every time I went and tried his utmost to make sure he did. He followed me around wherever we were so he could dart into the toilet after me, whether at home or visiting friends. In fact, he would think nothing of following me into public toilets. Even worse, he would sometimes push me into the gentlemen's.

The first time he did this, I was shocked at the disgusting state of them. It was true of all the men's toilets that I was pushed into over the years. They were filthy and extremely smelly, some with excrement smudged along the walls. Once in there, he would pull all of my clothes off and push me up against the filthy wall so he could force himself on me. He didn't always bother to get us into the cubicle. Sometimes, after his sexual appetite had been sated, he'd take all my clothes and run out with them, leaving me there naked. It was a real living nightmare.

I remember one time that he left me in the smelly men's toilet without my clothes and I hid in the cubicle, only to find it had no lock. I heard some men come in so I stayed crouched behind my door, sore from my husband's roughness and very frightened. I felt sure those men could hear the *thump, thump, thump* that I could hear in my chest, but when I thought I heard their footsteps fading, I peeped through the crack in the door. To my horror, a pair of dark eyes met mine across the latrine. It wasn't my husband. I didn't know if it was a coincidence that this stranger should be there looking at me or if he'd known I was there. Either way, I was petrified and pushed the door shut again, shaking with fear. A good few minutes must have passed before I dared to take another peep, but he was still there. All sorts of thoughts chased through my mind. Did I have to deal with two perverts instead of one? Was this all a set-up by my husband? Where was the nearest police station? And would I have the nerve to go in there with nothing on? Would I see anyone on the way who would recognise me? The humiliation of it all was too much to bear, and I even got to wondering if I would be killed before I reached the police station. I wished I were dead already. It was a wish I had almost every day of my married life.

After what seemed like hours of crouching there, I heard more footsteps approaching, and suddenly my clothes fell on top of me from over the door. Presumably from my husband, although he didn't say a word and I didn't hear him leave. I was still too terrified to move. The clothes were lying in a pool of stale urine next to me, but I was too frightened to put them on. I thought that as soon as I moved my weight from the door to dress myself, he would burst in—either my husband or the dark-eyed stranger. Then it would be sex—painful, violent, forceful sex. Rape. And possibly by both. I would die at the end of it, I was sure.

How I hadn't died on previous occasions was a mystery to me. I suppose something inside me always fought on, not for myself but for my children. I didn't know it was possible to sob so much and so silently inside that cubicle, but I continued like that for a long time behind the door. I wanted to plan what I would do when I finally got out of the toilets, but my brain would not budge beyond that door.

When I did slowly start to put my clothes back on, I attempted still to keep some weight against the door. It took me a long time, but once fully dressed, I stood up to force myself to peep, to see if the way was clear for me to get out. But before I could find the courage to look, I heard more footsteps approaching and the sound of someone urinating. I stayed there frozen, to give whomever it was time to leave. Time enough to come and go several times, probably. Then I peeped.

He was still there. The dark-eyed stranger was there, looking at me, and it definitely was no coincidence. I knew that now, though he still just stood staring as I ran smelly, damp, and degraded from my imprisonment. My husband was outside waiting for me. He grabbed me and then put his arm around me, just as if he loved me. I couldn't speak. I could hardly see or even think.

He was murmuring all the way home that he would look after me; he would clean me up and care for me. The walk home was not very far, but I do remember him leading me away from my place of humiliation in completely the opposite direction. I cannot remember any more about the journey home, but he probably had intercourse with me again somewhere along the way—by the river or in somebody's front garden (one of his favourite games). But for me now, it's totally blotted out. I do remember back at home in the kitchen him pulling my legs from under me, making me fall heavily on my back, then his big hands gripping me around my throat. Pulling my legs away in that manner was another favourite trick of his, and one time it resulted in a hospital trip and a support collar around my neck for a while. I told my friends I had fallen over. Eventually, I taught myself to fall without sustaining injury, although I often had to wear a polo-necked sweater to hide the handprints and bruising around my throat.

This particular time, we spent hours in the kitchen with him forcing himself into me, both front and rear, time and again. Eventually, he took me to the bathroom, sat me down, and ran me a warm bath. Then he bathed me gently, whispering soothingly as if to make everything all better. I must've drifted in and out of consciousness until finally he carried me up to bed, where I was allowed two or three hours sleep before getting up for the children. It was OK for him. He could sleep as long as he liked. He was out of work.

Other occasions followed a similar pattern, very often resulting in a visit to the local hospital. I had stitches in my head so many times that if I were to shave my hair off, it would look like a patchwork quilt. I had my nose broken, my teeth knocked crooked, and some minor fractures at various times. They knew me very well at our local hospital. I was so "accident prone" and always arrived with my "supportive and loving" husband by my side, teasing me about my clumsiness and making sure he was there when they administered whatever treatment was necessary. It puzzled me that no one there ever questioned why I was there week after week, but then I kept up the act too. "Yes, I've had another accident—silly me!" I'd say.

I wasn't only up at the hospital after "accidents". I was so desperately unhappy that I tried to take my life more times than I can remember. Usually overdoses. My husband always had a large supply of Distalgesic and paracetamol in the house. It wasn't a cry for help. I really wanted to die. My life was unbearable, and I had no one to turn to for support. Even to the few friends I was allowed, I never dared talk about the misery and violence. I kept up the pretence of being the female half of an extremely happy and devoted couple.

When I started taking overdoses, friends and neighbours thought (with encouragement from my husband) that I was becoming mentally unbalanced and treated me as such, even discussing my state of mind in my presence. I must have been in a zombielike state a lot of the time, due to the prescribed drugs I was taking. I was having my first breakdown by this time, while still struggling to look after my home and my first three children who were all under school age at this time. My youngest, Mark, was just a few weeks old. I became so ill that my husband was told I was not to be left alone. He was actually in employment at that time, working as a bus conductor for London Transport, so he invited a workmate's young girlfriend to lodge with us, keep an eye on me, and to administer my medication.

Until then, I could never remember whether I'd taken my tablets or not and in my confusion was sometimes taking a week's supply in one afternoon. So some of my overdoses at that time were in fact accidental. By then, I probably wasn't capable of doing anything like that deliberately. I wasn't capable of even thinking much either. I must have been on autopilot when caring for my baby. I would change and feed him when he cried, sometimes completely unaware that he'd had a nappy change and substantial feed not ten minutes previously.

When my husband brought 16-year-old Janice home to help, things improved slightly for a while. Janice was pleased to be staying with us. Being a typical teenager, she'd been looking for an excuse to leave home. Her single-parent father was a police officer, and I got the impression that he also kept up the role at home. Janice kept my tablets out of sight, handing me the required dose when due. Once my medication was monitored in this way, I started to get back to some semblance of a real person again. On seeing this, Janice gradually became relaxed about the situation, and when my tablets were due, she'd tell me to help myself from her handbag where she'd kept them. This was a big mistake. Within five minutes of helping myself to my tablets, I'd remember Janice saying they were due. I'd not remember having taken them so I'd go to her bag again and help myself to some more. Not just once but again and again until I passed out. So I'd be up at the hospital again.

My husband would never let me stay in hospital overnight though. He said he would take me home and care for me there. I was too afraid of him to argue, although the thought of staying in hospital away from my husband and having people caring for me was very appealing. But I knew it wasn't for me to have that care, rest, and safety. That was something that other people, real people, had when they were sick. It seemed to me that I wasn't allowed any love or care. I felt I didn't deserve it. I'd long since decided I was unlovable anyway.

I had my husband, my family, and my home—something I'd always wanted. But I just wanted to be a real person with a real, happy family life. Instead, I felt unloved, just a nonperson. Not of any use to anyone. And this was my lot.

CHAPTER 2

Childhood

AS A CHILD, I COULD never imagine anyone really loving me, although I'm sure my immediate family must have. My parents certainly looked after my sister and me to the very best of their ability and always did what they felt was right and proper for us. Some of my early memories are very happy ones in fact, such as my memory of the Co-operative Society's Summer Fete.

It was around 1957, and the fete was held at what used to be the Co-operative field in nearby Abbeywood. Our mother was a dedicated member of the Co-operative Society, always eager to collect her dividend when buying her groceries and support any of their events, such as the summer fete that year.

They were going to have a fancy dress parade for the children, and my mother went to great pains to make some original costumes for my sister, Hannah, and me to wear.

On the day of the fete, my mother dressed us both carefully and stepped back to admire her handiwork. Smiling proudly, she left the house with us arm in arm on either side of her, and we caught the number 96 bus to Abbeywood.

As a small child, I loved going out with my mother. At that time, she was a leader for the Pathfinders who met above the local Co-operative store. It was a club for the youngsters in the area—probably those whose mothers belonged to the Co-op. I felt that made my mother someone very important, and it made me feel important too when we went out with her. Sometimes she took the Pathfinders out on day trips, and she would take Hannah and me along. Hannah was lucky enough to be a member, being four years older than me, while I went instead to the local Playways club for the younger children.

The bus soon arrived at the venue, and we quickly joined the buzzing crowds already on the field and enjoying the entertainments.

First, we had a go at the coconut shy. Hannah and I were way off target. Our mother came very close, and we wanted her to keep trying. She said she might have another go later on. The thought of taking home a coconut for our father was quite appealing.

Hooking the ducks was good fun too. Not that I managed to hook any, but I think Hannah won a lollipop that she gave to me.

Then our mother stopped to have a chat with the Playways leader who'd arrived with her daughter Lucy. While they were chatting, I glanced across the field and noticed a small crowd of teenagers. The boys were rolling up their shirtsleeves and "whacking the rat" as the toy came hurtling down through the metal drainpipe. Another favourite game there. The girls were giggling and poking one another while calling encouragement to the boys. I watched those girls closely. I recognised them as my mother's Pathfinders. How I admired their full swishing skirts and petticoats! I would wear one too when I became a teenager, along with high heels and a ponytail. Then I would do rock and roll with the boys, and they wouldn't have to pick me up to twist me round because I'd be big enough to do it properly by then.

"Come on, girls. I'm dying for a cup of tea." My little bubble of dreams burst temporarily as we followed our mother to the tea and cakes stall. Hannah and I had some orange squash. We'd rather have had an ice cream, but our mother said we'd have to wait until after the fancy dress parade in case we messed up our costumes.

Suddenly, there was a loud thud, and I felt something brush against the back of my leg. I nearly spilt my squash. I turned around and brushed some dirt off my leg. A large Wellington boot lay just inches from my foot, and a spotty, red-faced youth was running to retrieve it, mumbling what I think were apologies. That was another favourite: the wellie throwing competition. We didn't have a go at that. We probably would've done worse than the spotty-faced boy.

At last, we heard over the loudhailer that it was time for the fancy dress parade to begin. Hannah and I joined the army of marching cowboys and Indians, fairies, soldiers, and nursery rhyme characters. We followed the procession around the field and past all the smiling mums and dads who were waving, calling, and darting forward to straighten collars or belts as their children marched past.

Our mother didn't need to do any of this. She just smiled warmly as we went by, seemingly confident of her handiwork. And rightly so. I don't remember now how I was dressed, but I will never forget my sister Hannah's costume as it was by far the cleverest idea of the day.

Our mother had spent a long time saving up her dividend tokens from the Co-op, and the week before the summer fete, a friend had drilled holes through all of the coinlike tokens. The next thing our mother did was to stitch through those holes and sew the tokens around the neck, waist, and bottom of a simple white tuniclike summer frock belonging to my sister.

Hannah looked lovely in anything she wore, with her dainty, slender figure and pretty, blonde curls, but on the day of the fete, she really looked a picture. There she was with her sash declaring, "Mummy's Little Bit of Divi"—the most original entry of all, and she won the first prize.

All these years later, I don't remember what her prize was, but to me, the best prize of all was the happy memory of the occasion. We did get our ice cream after the parade, and I think our mother even managed to win a coconut that we took home to our father at the end of the day.

But for all those days out, the annual seaside holidays, and the obvious care that was taken of us, I can't remember much in the way of cuddles or compliments. We did link arms cosily with each other when we walked down the road and always gave kisses goodnight, but I remember feeling strongly that my sister was very much the favourite. To my young mind, this was quite natural. She was, as I've already said, pretty, blonde, and dainty, with blue eyes and a clear skin. She was a good, sweet-natured girl, and she'd had a four-year head start to life. This meant that she was obviously four years brighter, four years more intelligent, and four years more sensible than me, and the pretty and dainty bits were a bonus.

I didn't think that I was pretty, and I certainly wasn't dainty or blonde. When I looked into my dressing table mirror, I saw a very unattractive girl looking back and wished it weren't me. I saw hair that I labelled "dog's muck brown" not to be funny but because that was how I really saw it. It never seemed to look nice either (possibly linked to the fact that our mother always cut our hair for us). I also saw blotchy, freckled, rough skin, and when I examined my features, I felt I was looking at a child with Down syndrome. I knew that I wasn't and it wasn't a nice thought to have but felt I had perhaps been born just one step away from it.

On into my teenage years, while my sister blossomed, I cultivated a bumper crop of spots along with lank and greasy hair. Whenever I went to my mother for comfort and advice about it, she'd tell me off for being vain. "Who's looking at you?" she'd question. Of course, I forgot. Nobody was looking at me. Nobody ever would. I tried my hardest to be a nice person inside, although I believed that nobody would get to see that far. The exterior would put them off before they got to the inside. I knew that was true because of the difficulties I'd had at my primary school.

I was virtually shunned by all the children. Not that I really wanted to be popular as that would mean they would have to look at me, and as my mother had so often pointed out, "Who's looking at you?" I knew I was ugly, and on top of that, I had a very rough, dry skin. Because of that, the children always used to taunt me, "She's got the lurgy. She's got the lurgy." And they never came even as near as touching distance from me if they could help it. When it came to lessons, such as PE or dancing, where we were required to work in pairs, no one would ever be my partner. I had to adapt the task to work on my own or partner with the teacher. The idea of boys and girls dancing together did seem quite exciting, and I knew if I had been one of the pretty girls, I would've loved it. There was one boy in my class called Terry whom I thought seemed really nice and very handsome. If I'd been Elaine Eversley or Susan Taylor, I could've been friends with him and perhaps even had him as my dancing partner. But no. I was me—Hilary Thrift—so I didn't bother to imagine or even dream a little bit about what it would be like to be friends with him. "She's got the lurgy" rang silently in my ears every time we had to pair up, and I stood alone at the side of the class.

In my first year at primary school, when dinnertime came, I thought this was my chance to escape and run home to my mum. My sister kept telling me that she wouldn't be there because she was at work. But I just couldn't grasp this. She was always there in the mornings when we left for school and always there when we came home again afterwards. To my young mind, I couldn't imagine our mother having any sort of a life in between, so when the infants' bell sounded for dinner, I'd be out of that classroom, down the corridor, and into the cloakroom. I'd grab my coat from its peg and run as fast I could through the playground and out of the gate to get back home. I never got very far though because minutes after our lunch bell was the juniors' bell. My sister would run out of her classroom, grab her coat from the cloakroom, and chase down the playground and through the gate after me. She always caught me up. (Of course, she had four years more running experience than me.) Then after the same unbelievable explanation about our mum away typing in an office, she'd grab hold of me and push me back through the dreaded gates and into school again.

As young children, our mother used to diligently make all of our clothes, and she had made us both beautiful, red, woollen coats with smart buttons and velvet collars. We must've looked a strange sight the day I grabbed the wrong coat and ran down the playground with it flapping around my ankles, while Hannah followed with her coat barely covering her bottom! After a while, the teachers got wise to my tricks and Hannah was allowed out of her class on the infants' bell so she had a better chance of catching me before I left the building.

When my sister was 11, in her last year at primary school, she went on holiday to Austria for a week with the leavers' class. She had a lovely time and brought me back a little Austrian doll that I treasured. I looked forward to when I got to the top year and would go too.

My sister was a bright girl, and our parents were very disappointed when she failed the 11-plus examination to go to grammar school. However, she did go into the highest grade at the local secondary school, and two years later, she passed the 13-plus exam and gained entry into the technical school. There, she took a secretarial course and later took CSE examinations. Mum and Dad were very proud of her.

I was proud of Hannah too—whatever she did. I loved and admired her unconditionally, almost to the point where I wanted to be her. When I was very small, I'd sit and watch her playing with her toys and dolls, then when she'd finished, I'd ask if I could have a turn playing with them.

"No. You'll break them," she'd say. "Play with your own."

But that wasn't what I wanted to do. I wanted to do what she'd been doing. I loved her and everything she did. So when she left the room, even though she'd said no, I'd set up the toys and dolls as she'd had them and start an identical game. At the time, I didn't feel that I was being bad or naughty, though to this day my family claims that I was a very naughty child. But the inevitable always happened. I was quite heavy-handed and something always got broken, and then I would be devastated. The sight of Hannah upset and crying was very distressing to me. I would say I was sorry as many times as I could and try to cuddle her, but she'd go and lock herself into the bathroom, crying. I'd be outside, calling, "Sorry," and banging on the door for her to come out. My mother would be extremely angry with her disobedient and disappointing daughter, so I'd receive a good hiding and some privilege withdrawn. But to me, the worst thing of all was to see my sister so distressed and be unable to make it up to her.

Meanwhile, the thought of the holiday to Austria when I reached leavers' year kept me going. I couldn't think of anything more exciting than that. Hannah had actually been away on another holiday without the family. She had been to Bexhill-on-Sea with the local youth club as well one year. I didn't get to join that club so that holiday wasn't an option, although I did secretly hope I might get to go on that one too somehow.

But age 11 came and went. Leavers' year came and went. Leavers' year holiday came and went. Without me. To this day, I still don't know why I didn't go. I supposed I wasn't good enough and didn't deserve to go. It was never debated or even mentioned, at least not in my hearing, and the immense feeling of disappointment after four years of anticipation has stayed with me down to this day.

I didn't pass the 11-plus exam either, but then my parents had told me they never expected me to. However, I did go into the top grade at secondary school, just as Hannah had. This must've surprised my parents, though I don't recall any reaction from them about it. Then when I was 13, I really surprised everyone. I passed the 13-plus, just like my sister had. My parents were amazed! They told me they had never expected me to pass.

Once I started at the technical school, I followed Hannah's lead and took the secretarial course. I always wanted to do what she did because she always seemed to know what was best, her being so clever (four years on me again). There was a big part of me that would like to have trained to be a teacher, particularly of English, my favourite subject. But Hannah was always right so I pushed that idea to the back of mind and got on with the shorthand and typing.

For all my unrecognised devotion to my sister, there were some occasions when I didn't listen to her. Somehow, whenever I stopped trying to be her and was me, doing whatever I decided to do, I always seemed to end up in trouble, adding fuel to the fire inside me that was saying what a bad, useless "nothing" person I was. And I just wanted to be a "real" person.

One quite vivid memory to illustrate this is from my preschool days when my mother did some child minding to supplement our father's income. Not only did I land myself in trouble, but also my mother's young charge, Peter, who must've been about the same age as me. We'd held hands tightly as we slipped unseen through the back gate. The street had never looked so huge to me before, and without Peter, it probably would've seemed even bigger.

"Peter, it's not that way." I tugged at his hand.

He still pulled away from me. "Look at that big motorbike."

"But we're going to the seaside. I know the way."

Peter then followed obediently.

I had been thinking about the seaside for a long time. I knew that we just had to go round the block and the seaside would be there. Like magic. It wasn't there in the wintertime or the cold weather, but it would be there today because the sun was shining and Peter and I were going. I did think it a shame that Peter hadn't got a bucket and spade like me. I supposed he could've taken Hannah's. She wouldn't miss them while she was at school, I thought, kicking the stones on the pathway.

Peter pressed his nose to a small hole in the fence beside us. "Have a look through here," he said.

"What's in there?"

"Nothing."

"Let me have a look then, Peter."

"Not yet. I haven't finished."

I sat down on my bucket. It wouldn't matter if we took our time. The seaside would still be there because the sun was still shining.

"Anyway, what's supposed to be in there? It's all grass. It's boring." Peter gave the fence a kick.

"Come on." I picked up my bucket. "We're going to the seaside." I took a quick peek through the hole before taking Peter's hand again. I thought everyone knew that my family lived opposite the school. My sister and I had often peeped through the holes in the fence to see the boys in their striped football kit. Another time I would tell Peter about them.

"Will you let me share your bucket and spade when we get there, Hilary?" he asked.

"I might. You could've borrowed Hannah's. Why didn't you ask?"

"Hannah wasn't there, and if she had been, she would've come with us and she would've wanted them," he replied matter-of-factly.

I thought about my sister then. I'd asked Hannah lots of times to come on this trip, but Hannah refused to believe the seaside was just round the block.

"Don't be so stupid!" she would snap. "Of course the seaside isn't 'just round the block.' It's miles away. And even if it was 'just round the block,' we wouldn't be allowed to go without Mum."

I never argued too much with my sister because usually she was right about things. But this time, I knew I was right, and the only way to prove it was to go. Not just on my own. I had to take somebody with me and show them, and Peter seemed to be the ideal person. He had to cooperate with me because he was the visitor and I knew what was what. It was my house, my street, and my seaside.

As we turned the last corner, I broke into a series of skips and jumps. My moment of triumph was approaching.

"Where is it then?" Peter frowned.

"We've got to go right to the end of the road for it," I assured him, though a small pang of doubt suddenly gripped my chest as I peered down the street. It didn't look any different than it normally did in the winter and cold weather.

Peter was still frowning and grumbling quietly. I screwed my face up to see if it would look any different. It didn't. My legs started to turn into blocks of wood, and something inside my chest was trying fiercely to jump out. Clearly, the seaside was not at the end of the road.

Tears of frustration dropped onto my cheeks and my voice came small and broken. "We just have to wait here for a minute."

I could hear Peter asking, "Why? What for? Where's the seaside?"

But I couldn't answer him. Peter kept scowling at me and asking me until I couldn't stand it any longer, so I just sat down on the pavement and howled. And Peter joined in.

The rest of the day passed in something of a blur. On looking back at the incident, I can vaguely remember a man in uniform taking us back to my mother, though I can't remember Peter ever coming to the house after that.

So where was the seaside then? Well, we used to go "just round the block". That was where we always went to catch the coach for our holidays.

CHAPTER 3

Teenage Angst

AS I SETTLED INTO LIFE at secondary school, I became aware that one by one all the other girls were acquiring boyfriends. Although ours was an all-girls establishment, our playing fields backed onto the local boys' school, the same one with its gates opposite our house. Lots of the girls linked up with those boys after school, walking arm in arm, smiling, and giggling. How I wanted to be one of those smiling, giggling girls coming in to school on Monday mornings with exciting tales of where I'd been with my beau.

Time went by, but none of the boys ever looked twice at me. No boy even looked once. But then I was more or less the only girl in my year still wearing short socks. Other girls my age were parading round in stockings and blue eyeshadow. I felt very old-fashioned and hated being the odd one out. I did complain to my mother and beg to be allowed to wear stockings but always got scolded for daring to ask. The acne didn't help much either. "Who's looking at you?" came into play again.

I thought Hannah's life seemed much more exciting than mine. She didn't have any proper boyfriends, but she did have lots of friends—boys and girls—and I'd listen intently to everything I could persuade her to tell me about them. Where they went, what they did, where they came from, and so on. One name that Hannah mentioned a few times was Billy Smith. He was a year younger than my sister and lived in Bermondsey. I was impressed. I assumed that anyone coming from London must be quite somebody. I learned that he was a slim boy with dark skin and black hair, and on the basis of this brief description, I built an image of a lean, Latin-type Romeo, imagining him to be kind, gentle, and softly spoken. I fell in love with the image I had. The next thing I did was to imagine he was one of my friends, and then I gradually came to imagine he was my boyfriend. This was not only in my imagination, but I also pretended to my classmates that it was true. In fact, in my own mind, I thought it was true. I felt I practically knew him and that when we finally did meet, it would all happen just as I'd imagined. So although I was never one of the smiling, giggling girls with their boyfriends after school, I did go in on Monday mornings with exciting stories of how my romance with Billy was progressing.

I kept this up for weeks, and my "romance" went from strength to strength while the other girls' boyfriends came and went. I felt that my "boyfriend" was by far the nicest of them all and that it was only a matter of time before I would really meet him and it would all really happen. So the sooner I could get to meet Billy Smith, the sooner the stories wouldn't be lies anymore and my conscience would be clear.

Round about this time, one of my mother's friends had promised to give me a signet ring. I got quite excited about this. Lots of girls at school wore rings. Some wore signet rings while others wore rings that they said were their grandmothers' engagement or wedding rings—some sort of family heirloom with sentimental value. Some girls claimed that their boyfriends had given them rings. I wished that Billy Smith would give me one.

However, when my mother's friend Doreen told me that she had a signet ring for me, I was overjoyed. Then I told the girls at school that Billy had promised to buy me a ring and every Monday morning they would crowd round to see if I'd got it. When they saw I still hadn't, they'd go off sniggering. I knew they didn't believe that Hilary, the clumsy, freckly girl in short socks, really had a gorgeous boyfriend from London. *I'll show them soon*, I thought as I described our latest romantic stroll by the River Thames.

Every time I saw Doreen, I wondered if she'd brought the ring. I was very shy and didn't like to look at her in case she could see just how eager I was for it, and then she would think I was greedy and not give it to me. I couldn't risk that. I'd set my heart on having that ring. I'd always wanted a signet ring, and while the anticipation over the weeks became almost too much to bear, it became, apart from Billy, the most important thing in my life.

The weeks turned into months, but still no ring came from Doreen. I couldn't remind her, and I couldn't say anything to my mother or she would call me greedy and grasping. I started to wish that I hadn't mentioned it to the girls at school as they had now started openly calling me a liar. This upset me dreadfully because I had always prided myself on my honesty. My mother was a highly principled religious woman and had brought us up to be the same. In fact, Hannah and I regularly accompanied her to her local Bible meetings and larger conventions farther down in Kent two or three times a year.

My sister sometimes used to go off for the day to other Bible conventions in London, where she'd meet up with her friends. I would look forward to her coming home in the evening to listen to her chat about them. Especially about Billy Smith, who I was glad to hear never seemed to have any steady girlfriend. This surprised me because he was absolutely gorgeous. Hannah said she wasn't keen on him when I asked, but she was a year older than him so I supposed she wouldn't be. (He was saving himself for me of course, though he didn't know it!)

One day Hannah said she would take me with her to one of the London conventions. I was so excited. She didn't normally take me anywhere if she could help it. At last I was going to meet all these grown-up, exciting friends that until then I'd only heard about. And Billy Smith would be there. I told all the girls at school that I had a really big date with Billy that weekend. I didn't tell them where. They would have laughed and mocked if they'd known it was to a religious gathering.

The week before we were due to go, I could think of nothing else but the convention and especially Billy Smith. I knew that after our eventual meeting, my life would take an upward turn. My schoolwork suffered all that week; I could hardly keep my mind on my lessons. Maths, geography, and even my favourite, English, all went out of the window compared with thoughts of the weekend that lay ahead of me. I planned out what I would wear, over and over again, and Hannah promised to do my hair in a more grown-up style on the day.

Saturday morning came, and I awoke with the most excited feeling deep in the pit of my stomach. When I got out of bed and looked in my dressing table mirror, I discovered that I had the biggest spot ever, just above the bridge of my nose, exactly in between my eyebrows. The excited feeling turned into one of bitter disappointment and upset. My sister put some of her make-up on me to try to cheer me up. I'd never worn make-up before. Then she backcombed my hair and fluffed it all out into a new and grown-up bouffant style, and she lent me a pair of stockings. She told me I looked at least 16. Then we set off to London on the bus.

The day went quite slowly. Hannah and I took notes during the discourses, which were interesting and informative, and we knew our mother would want to see them. But before the discourses began, during the lunch break and afterwards, I felt very uncomfortable. I knew the spot was still there and kept my head lowered to the floor in the hope that my fringe would hide the blemish. I also kept going off to the ladies' washroom to check on it. But every time I looked in the mirror, it was still there, flashing out at me like a Belisha beacon. My hair had gone lopsided and my lipstick had worn off. I might as well have gone in my short socks.

Hannah introduced me to some of her friends. I think I mumbled a hello to them, but I still kept my face towards the floor, only looking up once we'd moved away and were at a safe enough distance to get a look at them. I really just wanted to be back at home and in my, where I could be myself and no one could look at me. But the day seemed endless. I knew there were still a good few hours to get through before I could get home and be myself.

Coming home on the bus afterwards, I told Hannah that I had a headache so we didn't have to chat and kept my eyes closed so I could reflect on the day's events. I realised that these young people were Hannah's friends and had nothing at all to do with my life—and probably never would. And as for Billy Smith—I didn't even want to think about him. I hadn't been able to bring myself to mention him to my sister, let alone ask to be introduced. But from a distance, I had been able to work out which youth was him. He was dark, yes, with a vast mop of greasy, black hair, and yes, he was slim. He was as skinny as a matchstick, and with a face so thin as to look almost deformed. And he was very, very small. My romance had ended.

Back at school on Monday, I kept my head lowered still. Partly because of the spot, but mainly because I didn't want anyone to ask about my weekend. And nobody did. My romance had died, and I was back to being a nothing person again. I had nothing to talk about or share with the other girls, so I kept myself to myself from then onwards.

Several weeks after the trip with my sister, we were due to have our own convention in Kent. Fortunately, by then the offending spot had cleared up, although as always, there were plenty more elsewhere on my face to make up for it. I had always looked forward to these gatherings as it was something other than our usual routine. We always travelled by train, so at each station we'd be hanging out of the window looking for familiar faces and friends going to the same place. The nearer we got to our venue, the more crowded the train would get, and we'd be laughing and singing and catching up on news, as we'd only see each other two or three times a year at convention times.

This particular occasion started off no differently from any of the previous conventions. For the discourses, Hannah and I sat on either side of our mother, taking notes. About halfway through the afternoon, I excused myself out of necessity to go to the toilet. While washing my hands afterwards, I noticed that someone had left two rings on the side of the washbasin, and one of them was a signet ring. I was immediately reminded of Doreen and the promise she'd made to me several months earlier.

I wonder what a signet ring would look like on my finger, I thought.

I looked around, but apart from me, the washroom was empty as the discourses were still in progress. I felt it wouldn't hurt just to see and placed the ring on my finger. It fitted exactly and looked wonderful. But immediately, I took it off and placed it back on the washstand. The other ring was very pretty. It was a sweet, dainty ring with a diamond in the middle and smaller ones clustered around it. I wondered what that one would look like on and gently pushed it over my finger. I preferred the signet ring. The diamond one was much too dainty for my chubby hand.

But then the worst thing imaginable happened. I couldn't get this ring back off. I struggled with it for several minutes until my finger was red and swollen, but it was stuck fast. I hadn't wanted anyone to know that I'd been as vain as to try them on, let alone get one stuck, and I knew I'd be in the most terrible trouble if my mother found out. I'd already been much longer than I should have in the toilets, and that would be bad enough. I slunk back to my seat with my head lowered and my right hand clutching the left to hide the ring and swollen finger. It did hurt. I felt sick inside too, and the good feeling of the day was ruined.

I managed to keep the ring hidden from my family for a week. I always kept my hands out of sight anyway, thinking they were too rough and unsightly to be on show. No one noticed at school either, although no one at school took any notice of me now anyway. The sick feeling stayed with me all week. I really didn't want that ring on my finger.

But the following Sunday afternoon, my mother noticed the ring at teatime and asked me about it. I casually replied that it was one that Hannah had given me. She queried that, and Hannah said it wasn't, but I assured her I thought it was one of Hannah's. My father said nothing. He was always a quiet man, letting my mother take the lead, which she was happy to do. No more was said that afternoon, and I kept my hand more carefully out of the way. All that week, I had been secretly trying to remove the ring, but it wouldn't budge. I just wanted to get it off and dispose of it somehow, but it wasn't to be.

I didn't have to keep my hand hidden for long though. The next day, my mother noticed that I was still wearing the ring and wanted to know why I was wearing it on a school day. I had to come clean then and admit that it was stuck. Straight away she smothered my finger in green Fairy washing-up liquid.

"That will get the ring off," she assured me.

But it didn't. Next, she greased my finger generously with Vaseline and had another go at pulling it off. My finger was red and swollen again while the ring stayed put, so we had to abandon our attempts. She said we would have another go the next morning when the swelling had gone down. I went off to the safety of my bed and cried myself to sleep.

All attempts to remove the ring the following day came to nothing, so it was decided that I would have to be taken to a jeweller after school and have it cut off. I was terrified of that idea. I had a mental vision of my finger being cut off at the same time or at the very least a lot of pain and blood. It was bad enough too that some stranger would be scrutinising my hand and finger. Later that day, the deed was done at the local jewellers. Thankfully there were no severed fingers and no blood spillage.

But that was still not the end of the business. A few days later, my mother took me to a house where three of the local head men from our Bible group were waiting for me. I had no idea what they wanted with me and felt quite frightened. I couldn't grasp what they were talking about at first, and I just wanted to cry. But when I did realise what they were saying, it was as much as I could do to stop the tears from coming. They were questioning me about the ring. Apparently, it was an expensive engagement ring belonging to some poor, distraught young lady. I had always wanted to be a nice, good, kind person and just could not tell them what had happened, especially with my mother in the next room.

But the evidence was there, and the following week it was announced at my mother's Bible meeting that Hilary Thrift was excommunicated from the group. So at just 13, I was branded a thief and a liar, and no one was allowed to speak to me. My mother still took me to her meetings and the conventions, but while others were chatting and laughing with their friends in between discourses, I had to sit alone and silent at the back of the hall.

This carried on for a year. I wasn't allowed out anywhere without my mother now, and she complained bitterly that she couldn't do even half the things that she wanted to as she felt she had to keep me with her all the time, except for school of course. I wasn't allowed in anyone's house either (who knew what I might pinch next?) so that meant her social visiting was also very restricted, which she constantly reminded me of. Having no friends at school either, it was a very lonely year. I felt as if I were living in my own private prison.

I was so desperately lonely that I turned to the only person left. I prayed to God. I prayed every day, for a very large part of the day, and God must've got to know me very well that year. I even prayed at school in the break and at lunchtimes, as that was also a part of my "prison" that I found difficult.

This was at my first year at the technical high school for girls, and that year, the first years were based at the high school's annexe. This was Hall Place, a sixteenth-century manor house set farther out in the countryside, with grounds that were vast and beautiful. In these grounds at lunchtimes, groups of girls would sit around their transistor radios, tuned in to Radio Caroline, and listen to the Swinging Blue Jeans, the Hollies, and the Beatles while comparing homework and discussing boys. Much as I liked the music, I was never included in their groups.

When I prayed to God in these gardens, I felt at my closest to him, knowing that he had created all that beauty for our benefit. There was a small rippling river flowing along the left side of the garden from the house, with bridges leading to open fields on the other side. There was a topiary close to the building with chickens, horses, lions, and the like, all cut precisely out of the hedges. Next to the topiary was a rose garden with every colour rose imaginable growing there. In spring, the gardeners used to spread manure on the rose beds and the smell would waft up to our classrooms, where we'd all be wrinkling our noses at the stench.

Around the sides of the house were several of the ugliest, strangest-looking gargoyles staring out at us from the stone walls. Farther away from the house were stone steps leading down to a sunken garden. I found this garden particularly fascinating, and as most of the other girls stayed up near the house, I thought of this as my own secret garden. It was very pretty and colourful with arches of roses all around.

Behind this was a herb garden full of many different and interesting scents. Mint, rosemary, thyme, lavender, and many more that I couldn't recognise.

Finally, tucked away at the very back of the garden was the finest rockery I have ever seen. Sadly, since then, the rockery has been moved to another part of the garden to make way for a motorway. These were the beautiful surroundings I had during my year in "prison".

On the other side of the road from the manor house was a grassy slope stretching back up to town and to the bus home. It was quite a big hill, and I used to go up by bus until I discovered that if I walked the long trek up that hill, I could save money from the bus fare. And that meant that when I reached the top, I could afford to buy a chocolate bar in the sweet shop before getting the next bus home.

This went on for some weeks, and I felt very proud of myself for being so enterprising. So proud in fact that one day I told my mother. I wanted her to know how clever I was. But I didn't get the response I had hoped for. She was very annoyed with me. "All that money I've been giving you for bus fare, and you've been wasting it on sweets. I could've saved that money." She stopped giving it to me, so I had to do the long trek up the hill whatever the weather, with no chocolate reward at the top.

Other girls from school went in the shop every afternoon, and in front of the counter was a tray full of penny sweets. I'd noticed that a lot of the girls would pick up a handful of these sweets and slip them into their blazer pockets without paying for them. I still felt resentful that I now had to go up the hill every day with no sweets at the top, and one day after my trek, I took myself into the shop and picked up a sweet. Just one. Then I put it in my pocket without paying the penny and went for my bus home.

When I got off the bus at the end of my journey, the sweet was still in my pocket. It was still there the next day when I went to school. It was still there too when I trudged back up then hill at the end of that day. When I reached the top, I went quietly and trembling into the sweet shop, put my hand in my pocket for the sweet, and slipped it back into the tray, praying that no one would see. On coming out of the shop, I caught bus back home, holding back an ocean of tears that threatened to come.

Of course, attending the Bible meetings at this time was especially difficult for me because everyone there knew how bad I was, and that really hurt. My mother was obviously ashamed of me and resented the restrictions it put on her. Things must've got a bit better for her when we all got bicycles. It meant we could ride to the meetings together, and afterwards I could cycle straight home, leaving my mother there to chat with her friends. I didn't enjoy riding with my mother anyway, knowing how disappointed she was in me, and I quite enjoyed cycling home by myself.

It seemed to me that she'd always felt disappointed in me, even before the episode with the ring. At least the solitary ride home gave me the opportunity to do some more praying from my "prison".

One afternoon I came out of the meeting to find my bicycle had a flat tyre. I was very upset, stood beside my bicycle, and cried, waiting for my mother to come out. While I was waiting, a young man came out of the hall and spotted me.

"What's up, Hilary?" he asked, raising his eyebrows.

"You're not supposed to talk to me," I replied.

But he was not to be deterred. "I can't go home and leave you there crying. That wouldn't be very Christian, would it?" He fetched a pump from his car and pumped the tyre back up for me while I waited, feeling embarrassed and terrified someone would come out and catch him. I was very grateful to him though and relieved when he'd finished so I could get on home nearer to the safety, warmth, and comfort of my bed.

That year of imprisoned silence seemed like the longest year of my life. Of course, I never did get the ring from Doreen either.

CHAPTER 4

Bicycles and Scooters

THINKING ABOUT THE BICYCLES, I clearly remember the time that my mother went into Halfords in Bexleyheath and bought the biggest saddlebag in the shop.

Mum, Hannah, and I all rode bicycles at that time, though our mother's was more than just a means to get from A to B. She used it as a carrier for all the bits and pieces she picked up on her way. Bits and pieces that to my mind even Steptoe & Son would've turned down. Hence the purchase of the giant saddlebag.

She would knock on anybody's door if she saw something that looked remotely useful lying abandoned in their front garden. Like the time she knocked on the door of the parsonage in Wickham Street. I had to wait by the bicycles while she went in and enquired about a large piece of carpet rolled up by their dustbin. She hadn't bought the saddlebag yet so we had to take our bikes home first then come back and carry the carpet home between us. That was one time out of many when I wished I were invisible, especially when we walked past the White Horse Inn where Justine Cartwright, one of my classmates, lived. She might just have been looking out of the window at that moment.

Once my mother had acquired the saddlebag, there was no stopping her. On the way home from shopping, she would invariably come across some pieces of coal or the odd potato lying in the road, or lumps of firewood, or even pieces of string, and they would all be gathered up and tucked in the saddlebag, alongside the groceries.

Then there was the time I was cycling home from the library and noticed a beetroot lying in the road. My first thought was *If I were Mum, I'd pick that up,* and I almost stopped. But then I thought, *I'm not Mum,* and I promptly rode my bicycle through the middle of it with a big bump, laughing as I did so.

I arrived home a few minutes later to find my mother sorting through her shopping. "I'm sure I bought a beetroot down at Biddle's just now."

I actually told her what I'd done, though not until some thirty years later when I thought we could have a good laugh about it. And she still gave me a lecture on being thrifty!

When I was 14, our mother borrowed some money and purchased a motor scooter. A yellow Cento Lambretta 100cc. She borrowed the money from a close family friend, and between them, they drew up a proper agreement in front of another friend and signed it along with their witness. My mother liked to do things properly.

In readiness for her driving test, Hannah and I took it in turns to quiz her from the Highway Code book. She always got the questions right, and Hannah and I decided she must have a photographic memory. I looked forward to when she would pass her test so I could have a ride on the back of the scooter instead of going everywhere by pushbike.

My sister rode a small moped now that had originally belonged to our mother, bridging the gap between bicycle and motor scooter. Since Hannah had left school, she rode to her office job in London every day on the moped. I thought she looked really something zooming off in her warm jacket and high boots, her long blonde hair flying out from the back of her goldfish bowl crash helmet.

It seemed an eternity before the time came for our mother to take her driving test. Hannah and I went as usual to work and school respectively but rushed home eagerly at the end of the day to find out if she'd passed.

Over a cup of coffee round the kitchen table, our mother told us how she'd done. I didn't quite follow what was what, except when she told us about the emergency stop. The procedure was that the instructor would hide in the bushes along the lane in Abbeywood where she was taking the test. Then she would ride along the lane, keeping to the speed limit. Next, the instructor was to jump out from the bushes on to the pavement, and she was to do her emergency stop. But what actually happened was that she drove all the way down the lane, the instructor leapt out, but Mum was concentrating so hard on driving properly and keeping to the speed limit that she never even saw him! We told her she was lucky that she hadn't run him over. Surprisingly, she still passed the test.

I quite enjoyed going on the back of the scooter. I needed a bit of speed and excitement to spice up my life a bit, I thought. It would only be thirty miles per hour speed, but it was still fast and exciting compared to the pushbike.

By this time, I had been reinstated into the Bible group, so my mother had her freedom back and people were talking to me again. Nobody spoke about the incident that had led to my isolation, and it was never mentioned again amongst my family either. I got used to being a part of the group again, although I certainly didn't feel as if I was the same as everyone else and still felt the waves of my mother's disapproval.

Several weeks after my mother's passing of the long-awaited driving test, another weekend convention was scheduled. She said we'd drive up together on the scooter, and I was very excited because we would have to travel to the other side of London this time. Up until then, the rides on the back of the scooter were strictly local.

Early that morning, armed with Bibles, notebooks, and lunch, we set off eagerly, wearing our best clothes and our peaked crash helmets. Pillion riding along the main roads, sometimes as fast as forty miles per hour, was quite exhilarating. I wished I could abandon my crash helmet and feel the wind blowing through my hair. It wasn't the law to wear crash helmets back then, but it was mother's law, so the helmets stayed put.

It was raining a little bit but we were well wrapped up, and it didn't spoil the thrill of the ride. I knew my mother was very capable.

She didn't see the oil on the road as we passed the petrol station. Probably she was not experienced enough to recognise the danger. Suddenly we were spinning round like an out-of-control fairground ride. It was far too fast for any thoughts to go through my head, and by the time I realised what had happened, I was sitting up on the kerbside feeling very dazed. My mother was lying in the road with the scooter on top of her, and a small group of people had bunched around her. Then they were helping her, someone either side of her, leading her limping into the garage, with someone else pushing the scooter behind them. I was on my feet by then, and someone was calling to me "phone for an ambulance!" So I stumbled off and found some offices where they were very helpful and made the phone call for me.

My mother was sorted out at hospital. No serious damage, fortunately, just cuts and bruises. The scooter was OK too, and we still managed to get to the convention later on that day.

I hadn't been physically hurt, though if I had, no one would have known. No one took the slightest bit of notice of me at the time of the accident. No one asked if I was all right even. It had been almost as if I wasn't really there—just a nothing person.

I did actually have a few minor bruises, and I had a dull headache that lasted a year and made me extremely miserable. I never told anyone. After all, who the heck was I to think that anyone would want to know?

My father didn't drive. Our mother said that he did drive a tank in the 1939–1945 war, but he never spoke about the war and never drove afterwards. He did occasionally ride pillion with our mother, but not often. (He wasn't a religious man so very rarely came to the group meetings or conventions with us.) Apparently, he was a very nervous passenger, our mother said, and told us that he would put his arm out when they were about to turn a corner. She kept telling him not to because she saw to all the hand signals, but he still did, and one day in his enthusiasm, he knocked a cyclist clean off his bicycle!

At the age of 16, I applied for a provisional driving licence, and my mother taught me to ride the scooter. I thought I was going on to greater things. I had very little opportunity to practise though, because it was still my mother's main form of transport.

Once I took the scooter out on my own, daringly without my crash helmet and without my mother's knowledge. It was the era of the mods and I rather fancied myself as one of them, with their smart style, their parka jackets, and their decorated scooters, all done up with chrome, fur seat covers, and flags. Of course, our little Lambretta didn't sport any of these extras, any more than I owned a parka, but I liked to pretend. (My original dream of being a teddy girl on reaching my teens was completely washed up. They'd gone right out of fashion along with their flared skirts and ponytails.)

The alternative to the trendy mods were the leather-clad, motorbiking rockers. They were a tough crowd and could be quite frightening when roaring down the road in vast gangs amidst clouds of smoke. The mods and rockers were sworn enemies, and on bank holidays, they would all bike down to Margate for seafront battles that had to be broken up by the police and would be seen later on the six o'clock news by all who were privileged to own a television.

Before the mods drove to Margate, the ones in our area all used to meet up at the Twisted Wheel, a small coffee bar along the High Street opposite the Granada Cinema (neither of which exists today), and there they would discuss tactics before the convoy left. I never went into the Twisted Wheel, much as I would like to have done, but I would imagine what it would be like to sit in there while sipping coffee and listening to the jukebox with the other girls, all in our smart gear, while our boyfriends made their plans before whisking us all off on the backs of their fur-seated scooters. Our arms would be wrapped tightly around our partners' waists as we set off towards the coast for some excitement. Tough as the enemy rockers were, the mods were a pretty cool bunch and always managed to hold their own.

But I wasn't a mod, and I wasn't drinking coffee in the Twisted Wheel, and there was no parka-clad boyfriend, so I did the next best thing. I pretended. Only this time, I kept it to myself. Then off I went on my mother's scooter, minus my crash helmet. In my head, I was humming the Who's latest hit record, which seemed to have become an anthem for the mods. I drove around the local streets until I caught sight of a dozen or so mods coming towards me on their scooters. I stopped as they passed, then turned the scooter around and tagged on the end of the posse. They didn't notice, but that didn't matter. I pretended. To the sound of "My Generation" in my head, I was one of them, riding my scooter, the wind blowing through my hair, without a care in the world. It felt wonderful.

I hadn't gone far when I heard a little *pop pop pop* and saw my very angry mother flagging me down from the moped. "Where are you going? Who are these boys? Where is your crash helmet?"

Another dream over. Back home I went in disgrace. I wouldn't bother with that dream anymore, and I didn't ride the scooter much after that either.

My mother, surprisingly, encouraged me to keep it up, and as I was still quite new at it, she took me out one afternoon to a local car park where she thought there would be a lot of space for me to practise. I rode around the car park several times while my mother watched and directed. Then, as I was manoeuvring the bike and getting really confident with it all, I saw that I had got much too close to a parked car and needed to apply the foot brake, which I did. Or rather, I didn't because there was a big bump. I didn't stop, and the scooter careered into the side of the parked car. I was so sure I had applied the brake. I couldn't understand it.

My mother, of course, was very angry and whisked me back home quickly before anyone noticed. I decided then that I must be totally stupid to really believe I had braked when I obviously hadn't. If it happened once, I thought, it could happen again.

I never rode the Lambretta after that.

CHAPTER 5

First Love

A VERY IMPRESSIONABLE AGE FOR any young, healthy female and me: 16. That was when I fell in love.

My mother had trusted me to go away for a weekend with my very sensible friend Marlene. Had it been with anyone else, I don't think I'd have been allowed to go, and the fact that we were going to a religious convention must have been the redeeming factor for our weekend.

It was the first time I'd ever been away from my home and family, so with overwhelming excitement, I boarded the coach with my friend. I don't know if Marlene had been away from her family before, but she sat beside me on the green and purple striped seats, hands in her lap, as if a coach journey to Wiltshire was something we did every weekend. I could hardly sit still.

We stayed the two nights in a small, cosy bed and breakfast house, the two of us sharing a double bed. I can remember clearly lying on my back on the bed last thing at night, waving my slim legs in the air, much to the irritation of my plump friend next to me. I can remember explaining to her, "I always do this before I go to sleep." I'm sure I'd never done it before in my life. It's certainly strange what the excitement of newly discovered freedom can do to a 16-year-old.

The convention itself went well, with interesting and upbuilding discourses, heart-stirring songs and prayers, and properly organised meals served in marquees at lunchtimes.

Then there was Gary. Golden-haired, blue-eyed, beautiful Gary. He lived in Swindon and was there both days at the local football stadium where the convention was being held. He was the brother of a friend of another friend, and I was introduced to him casually on the first morning we were there. He was the most handsome young man I had ever laid eyes on.

I was extremely shy then of boys having no brothers and a very quiet father and having attended all-girls schools from the age of 11. It didn't come easily to me to be friends or make small talk with the opposite sex, but somehow with Gary, it was different. Normally boys didn't notice me, but once introduced, he looked straight at me, into my eyes, and I looked right back into his. And as we spoke comfortably together, I was conscious of a new and wonderful feeling deep down inside.

Then Gary had to leave the stadium to collect a friend. He assured me he was coming back and would see me later. I did some speedy thinking anyway and came up with an idea to make sure he did. I asked him to bring me back a packet of tissues from town. He agreed and wouldn't even take the money I offered him.

My new friend owned a smart motor scooter, not with added chrome and fur like the mods of the time, but I was very impressed anyway as I watched him drive off towards the town. The reason I was so impressed was that Gary had a disability. He had an artificial leg. As a young child, his own leg had been amputated because of disease. A wooden one had been fitted and renewed regularly as he grew, with the promise of a metal one at 21, an age at which a young man was considered fully grown.

I did see him again that weekend. When he returned from the town, he came to find me with the tissues just as I'd hoped. I was sitting right at the top of the football stand when he spotted me.

"Stay there!" he shouted. "I'm coming up!"

And he did. I waited a long time as he climbed every one of the rickety, wooden steps at the back of the high stand. We sat for a long time there getting to know each other before he left me to join the friend he'd picked up from town.

Over the weekend, I saw Gary several times, and each time, the new and wonderful feeling grew. But as all good things do, our weekend had to come to an end.

I cried all the way home when Marlene and I left Swindon, even though Gary came to wave us off at the coach station. I watched through the back window until he was a small dot in the distance while Marlene sat, hands in lap, tutting and rolling her eyes.

After that, the new and wonderful feeling turned to hollow emptiness and I never saw him again.

Perhaps if we'd met a few months earlier, things might have been different because, although it seemed to me that there was an obvious attraction and closeness between us, he was already committed. When we had sat together at the top of the football stand, I had learned a lot about him. He'd felt, possibly quite unjustifiably, that he'd grown up in the shadow of his older brother and wanted to prove himself just as much a man, regardless of his disability. The only way he thought he could do this was to marry and have children, so he courted the first young lady who took notice of him. Her name was Lesley. She was four or five years his senior and was the friend he'd collected from town that weekend. She was his fiancée. Our religious beliefs made us feel a strong sense of commitment in that it would be unthinkable for Gary to break off the engagement.

I did casually ask the friend of a friend about him from time to time, and the reply usually came back that he'd been asking about me too. I could've asked that friend of a friend to get his address so I could make contact, but I knew she would've disapproved, being of the same faith and following the same strong principles as us.

My secular work then was as a secretary for a small family firm of self-adhesive tape stockists. When I returned to work after our weekend, my boss's wife was very sympathetic to my feelings. She had me looking in telephone directories and telephoning the directory enquiries number in an attempt to trace his family and planning out letters I could write to Gary when we did. I don't know if I'd have had the courage to ever write to him, but I'll never know because we never did manage to trace his address.

When I heard he'd got married, I stopped asking about him and tried to put him out of my mind, but even though I married Jim a few years later, I couldn't forget Gary.

After I'd been married for two or three years, something prompted me to ask about him again. Probably because my own marriage was a disaster, my thoughts strayed back to someone I thought I'd loved and would've been happy with.

This time, I didn't get the reply that he'd asked about me. The reply I did get though came as a huge shock. My friend told me that after he'd got married, he and Lesley had moved into a lovely cottage just outside Swindon. When he'd reached 21, he'd had his metal leg fitted, but shortly afterwards, while seeing to an electrical repair in his home, he received a severe electric shock. The metal of his new leg had acted as a conductor and the shock killed him instantly. Six months later, Lesley had remarried.

I don't know what shook me more: the news of Gary's death or the fact that Lesley had remarried so soon. I cried for weeks afterwards, all the if-onlys going through my head.

Once I'd got over the initial shock, I felt more comfortable and less guilty thinking about him. He became my imaginary hero. When my husband was cruel to me, I would run upstairs, and in my mind's eye, Gary would be standing at the top of them, arms outstretched, and I would throw myself into them. He'd guide me into my bedroom where we would sit on the bed, his strong, comforting arms engulfing me, while I cried my heart out against his chest. I'm sure it was the comfort I imagined he gave me that kept me going during those unhappy years.

Although we only met one brief weekend, Gary definitely played a large part in my life, and although no one can turn the clock back to change events, I'm still glad that I met him: golden-haired, blue-eyed, beautiful Gary, brother of a friend of a friend.

CHAPTER 6

A Working Girl

I STAYED ON AT THE technical school for an extra year of secretarial training. I wanted to get some qualifications like my sister had four years previously.

When I did leave school, I was overjoyed. My school days had never been particularly happy, so now was my chance for a new start.

Hannah helped me to find a job. She took me to a small place of business in our hometown, the boss of which was an ex-employee from where my sister worked up in London. He was very pleased to see Hannah again and introduced me as her little sister who had just left school and needed a job.

Yes, he said, he would employ me. I would be his secretary. It was such a relief to find a job so soon after leaving school.

It was a new business situated in an old Victorian house just a twenty-minute walk from our home. The only people working there were my boss and an elderly gentleman who came in three days a week to pack the orders up. The deliveries would then be made either by the elderly helper of by the boss himself. Before I joined the firm, apparently the boss's wife used to come down occasionally to do some paperwork and typing of letters.

My first morning there two weeks later was quite an event. This was my first ever job, and boy, was I green! I arrived at nine o'clock and Mr Ash, my boss, showed me around the building explaining what was what.

The office was in the front room of the house, and this was comprised of my boss's desk, a desk and typewriter for me, and some old filing cabinets that Mr Ash showed me how to use.

Next he showed me where all the stock was kept in the back two rooms, and stocked there were more types of tape than I knew were in existence. Not Sellotape—they were our rivals—but sticky tapes, electrical tapes, masking tapes, waterproof tapes, double-sided tapes, and so on. The list was endless. And every tape had a number that I had to learn.

Upstairs was my boss's home where he lived with his wife, Vera, and their two darling little girls, Sharon and Melissa. Just at the top of the stairs was the toilet that we all used, and behind that was their kitchen overlooking a small garden. I was allowed in the kitchen to make the tea and coffee whenever we felt thirsty. While we were upstairs, Mr Ash even showed me around the rest of their flat. That's when I first met his wife and children. I thought Mr Ash was around 50 while Vera could only have been in her 20s. She was very tall and elegant. I thought she looked like a film star.

Then he took me back downstairs to begin my training. As soon as we re-entered the office, the telephone started to ring.

"Go on," Mr Ash commanded. "Start your job. You answer it."

I think all the colour must've drained from my face. What would I say? How would I pick it up? We didn't have a telephone at home. I'd never answered a phone before.

No more was said. Mr Ash picked up the receiver. "Good morning. Ash Tapes."

That was it. That was all I had to say.

After the call finished, Mr Ash said that I was to answer the next call and say just that. Then, regardless of what the caller said, I was to say, "Hold the line a moment please," then pass the receiver over to my boss. What could be easier?

There wasn't anything else to be done at that moment so Mr Ash sent me upstairs to make tea. When I came back down with the two steaming mugs, there were two male visitors in the office, one of them perched on the edge of my desk. Mr Ash introduced them to me. They were both representatives for adhesive tape manufacturers, one from the manufacturer of the tape that we stocked and the other from the opposition. Both men were very friendly and dressed very smartly, and they were both very tall. I wondered if all reps were tall. Was that a requirement of the job? I felt very intimidated being the only female amongst these three smartly suited businessmen.

After introductions were made, they carried on talking business. I couldn't follow the conversation, knowing nothing yet about the tape business, so I sat drinking my coffee and fiddling self-consciously with the stationery on my desk.

Then, horror of horrors, in front of Mr Ash and the two visiting reps, the telephone rang.

It was my job. Mr Ash had said. That was why I was there.

"Good morning. Ash Tapes" was all I had to say.

But I had to pick it up first.

How?

Which end?

If I hesitated, would Mr Ash answer it again?

No. And no.

The office went silent, all but the continuous ringing of the telephone, and all eyes were on me. It was my job.

I made a grab at the telephone, the first time I had answered one in my life. I picked up the receiver and dropped it clumsily.

I scrabbled to the floor and retrieved the receiver, six eyes still following me.

"Hello," I quavered. What was I meant to say?

No one was answering, though I was aware of my boss and the reps laughing loudly and shouting instructions. "Other way up, girl!" "Turn it around!"

I must've looked a strange sight with the receiver in my hand and the curled lead spiralling out somewhere beside my left ear.

"Ash Tapes! Ash Tapes!" someone reminded me.

I flushed a deep pink and turned the handpiece around. I think I just managed to mumble, "Ash Tapes," into the mouthpiece, before thrusting the telephone at my boss, who thankfully finished the call. I was then dismissed to make more tea.

Later that morning when Mr Ash was upstairs and I was alone for a few minutes, I practised picking up the phone, getting the right end, and saying, "Good morning. Ash Tapes."

I did get the hang of it eventually, though I don't remember how long I was working there before I realised that after midday I had to change it to "Good afternoon."

On my first day, I ate my lunch of homemade sandwiches still sitting at my desk. Mr Ash said he would man the telephone for an hour so I could relax. I decided in future I would bring a book to read during my lunch break or to even take a short walk down to the shops.

Before I settled back to work, my boss asked me to pop next door to the confectionery shop to buy him a packet of twenty Players cigarettes. He also gave me some extra money for a bar of chocolate for myself. He did this on most days, and I really enjoyed my chocolate treat because at home we normally only had sweets on a Friday.

After he finished work at the end of the week, our father would go down to the Lovell Avenue sweet shop and buy a quarter of Merrymaids (a delicious toffee sweet with a chocolate coating). Then as a family, we would settle round the dining room table for a game of cards, Monopoly, or something similar, and he'd share the Merrymaids among us during the evening. I think he sometimes bought a bar of chocolate too as more than once I spotted a large inviting bar in the pantry. I never got any though, so I could only assume that my parents ate it after Hannah and I went to bed.

My mother gave it away once when she claimed that I could smell chocolate from upstairs. Apparently, after I'd been sent to bed as a youngster, I had a habit of making excuses to come downstairs again, worried I was missing out on something (probably the chocolate). After we had gone to bed, my parents often seemed to be laughing and giggling, so naturally I felt I was missing out!

Anyway, back to the office. I relished my daily chocolate bars and was only too willing to go to the shop for my boss. In fact, on the few days when he didn't send me, I felt almost cheated.

Mr Ash dictated a couple of letters to me on that first day, and I think he was impressed with my speedy use of shorthand. Then I typed them up for him to sign. I typed them both up four or five times before I got them just right, but I think Mr Ash was quite pleased with the final copies.

My last job of the day was to stamp the letters and take them to the nearby post office along with a small parcel of masking tape that had to be weighed and stamped. When I returned, Vera came downstairs with Sharon and Melissa. They all said goodbye to me, and the little girls kissed me on the cheek. It had been a good first day, despite a few mishaps, and I was learning.

Back at school in our last year, we'd had to write an essay on how we would spend our first week's wages once we were working. I loved English lessons and loved writing so I got all my ideas together for my essay.

First, I thought, I could buy some presents for my mother, father, and Hannah. Then I could buy myself some new clothes, some sweets, and some magazines. (The magazines would have to be kept hidden as my mother didn't approve of pop magazines—or girly comics with their stories of teenage romance.) Then a trip to the cinema with my sister would be good, and ice skating in London would be even better. Then with a bit of luck, I might have enough left over to start saving for a holiday. Oh, I had lots of ideas, and I wrote a really good essay including all of them.

At the end of my first working week, I was given my first ever wage packet, which back then contained the actual cash that had been earned. Plus Mr Ash pushed two half-crown pieces in my hand. A sort of extra tip, I supposed, for my good work. I didn't open the small envelope though as I was expected to take it home and give it straight to my mother. But I did have two half-crowns that she didn't know about.

I left the office, and instead of taking the short cut home through the back streets and under the railway bridge, I walked round the main roads where the shops were, thinking about how I could spend my two half-crowns.

As I passed the butchers, I had the best idea. Sausages. I loved sausages. They were absolutely my favourite dinner. I went into the shop and bought a pound of the butchers' own pork sausages. Then I came out clutching my prize.

The next thing to think about was eating them. I could take them home and cook them. But if I did that, I would be expected to share them with my family and I didn't want to do that. They were my sausages. I knew I would never get away with cooking and eating them in secret either, so after some brief consideration, I did the only other thing left to do. I ate them raw. Every single one of them I ate raw on the rest of my way home until all I had left was the empty greaseproof paper they'd been wrapped in, which I disposed of in the litter bin outside the chemists' shop.

When I arrived home, I handed my unopened wage packet to my mother, who tucked the contents away into her brown leather purse and gave me back a few shillings for myself, enough perhaps to buy a pair of stockings and a couple of chocolate bars.

As I learned the ropes of my job, I enjoyed it more and more. I became so confident with the telephone that in time I could handle the majority of calls myself. I could take orders, price them up according to quantity, check the stock, and then pack the orders up along with their advice notes that I'd typed up ready for delivery. I even learned to balance the accounts for Mr Ash and could handle most other office duties. In fact, my boss could go out all day and leave me to run the office single-handedly.

Several times when I had the office to myself, I had some fun with the telephone. We had a little yellow codebook from British Telecom so that we could dial anywhere without having to go through the operator service. It even gave the numbered codes for dialling abroad. Now that got me thinking.

One day, when nobody else was around, I dialled the code numbers for Germany, followed by a variety of other numbers chosen at random. It took quite a while to connect as I waited nervously on the edge of my seat. Eventually, I heard an unfamiliar ringing sound at the other end of the line—the German end.

"Guten morgen," I said proudly. I'd learnt German at school, and here, at last, was my chance to put it to use. "Ich bin Hilary. Du bist sie." I could not understand the reply and hung up hastily, giggling to myself.

I tried again, this time a different German number, chosen randomly. "Guten tag. Ich bin einer kleiner schulerin." I hung up quickly again. I'd had a German penfriend when I was about 13. I thought what a pity it was that we weren't still in touch. She may've been on the telephone at home or work by now too. But I still very naughtily amused myself by dialling random German numbers and practising a few brief phrases.

On looking back, I wonder now about the time difference. Was I waking people up from their night's sleep just to tell them I was a little schoolgirl or ask where my uncle's pencil was? Also, Mr Ash never queried the telephone bill when it arrived either.

Occasionally my boss's wife, Vera, would come down and ask me if I'd like to go upstairs for an hour or so to look after Sharon and Melissa and she would take care of the office. I loved doing that. They were such dear little girls. We would play together and I would cuddle them in turn. I thought how kind Vera was to let me do that. If they were my little girls, I didn't think I'd want to leave them for a minute.

When Sharon started going to ballet classes at the co-operative hall, sometimes Vera would ask me to go and collect her at three o'clock. If I got there a bit early, I could see the end of the lesson, a whole row of sweet little girls in tights and tutus kicking their legs at the bar. If I had little girls one day, I thought, I would send them to the co-operative hall to learn ballet too.

Yes, my job was quite varied and I was happy there. I could now hold my head up as a working girl.

CHAPTER 7

First Boyfriend

THROUGHOUT MY TEENAGE YEARS, NO other feelings came close to those that I'd felt that weekend in Swindon, and although I did have boyfriends after that, I never felt that heady, overwhelming magic with any of them.

My first boyfriend was called James, and he came on the scene when I was 17. He was about the same age as me and I met him through my friend Pamela, whom I used to go and stay with in Northfleet on the occasional weekend.

It was about a twenty-minute journey by train, and through my friendship with Pamela, I built up quite a good little circle of friends in that area, including James. Occasionally, we'd all get together for a party or a record session at the home of whoever's parents were the most long-suffering.

The parties were the most fun. By this time, the previously admired mods had gone out of fashion and it was now the day of the hippy, flower power, and peace. For these parties, we used to dress up in our flared trousers and platform shoes, with little cowbells tied around our wrists and waists. We girls thought we really looked the business and finished off our ensemble with freshly picked flowers clipped into our hair. Then we'd dance the night away to sounds, such as the Bee Gees' "Massachusetts" and Procal Harem's "A Whiter Shade of Pale" (or at least until eleven o'clock, when the party-throwers' parents sent us all home).

One of the lads in our group had a rather noticeable nervous habit. At very frequent intervals, he would whisk a comb out of his back pocket and flick it briskly through his quiff. I felt sorry for any girl who would become his girlfriend because I knew from experience that even when sharing a slow dance together, he would take his arm from his partner's shoulder, fish in his back pocket, and give his quiff a quick once-over. Nice as this lad was, I could never feel anything romantically for him for this reason alone.

I think my best memory of him comes from a trip we all made to Dreamland, Margate's very popular funfair. We all went up together by train, the journey itself, although taking up a large part of the morning, being all part of the fun. But what sticks fast in my mind is sitting beside this lad on the Big Dipper ride—at that time the most exciting ride of the fair.

I can picture it now: Our crowd is queuing eagerly, huddled and giggling in anticipation of the thrill. Then we are climbing into our seats in pairs. Next comes the slow climb up the first slope, where we are in eager expectation of the huge plunge ahead of us. As we reach the extreme height, ready for the drop, we are all holding our breath, ready for the long-awaited, biggest thrill of the fairground. And in the seat next to me, at this very moment, the lad whips out his comb and casually flicks it through his windblown quiff!

Nobody believed me when I told them, but it was true!

They were a good fun crowd, and after a few months, the aforementioned James and I started going out as a couple. We went out for about five months and I think I was his first girlfriend, so it was nothing very serious.

He was a nice, polite boy who was very clean and smart. In fact, as my mother once described him, he was fastidious. I wasn't sure if she meant that as a criticism or a compliment, but I liked him.

What spoilt it for me though was one weekend when we were invited to a party. I spent the latter part of the afternoon getting myself ready. A good strip-down wash in the bathroom, make-up carefully applied, especially the sultry mauve eyeshadow that had become my trademark. I dressed carefully in my best party clothes and brushed my hair. I backcombed it out and piled it up on top into loose curls, ready to add a few flowers should we come across any on our way. The piece de resistance was a really fashionable blouse that my mother had picked up at a jumble sale. It was dark purple with a two-inch-wide frill around the neck and down the front—the latest fashion.

Six o'clock came and James arrived ready to take me back to Gravesend for the party. I looked at him; he did look smart. He always did look extremely smart, but today he definitely looked too smart. He was wearing a dazzling white shirt with a three-and-a-half-inch ruff all the way down the front. It was obviously brand new. He'd probably spent the entire afternoon bathing and getting ready. He even smelt better than me!

We did go to the party, but it was the last time we ever went out as a couple. Fortunately, we parted as friends. He was a really nice boy but a bit too fastidious for me.

Two weeks after we had split up, I was very surprised to have him telephone me at the office where I worked. My boss did not encourage personal telephone calls and was in the office when James rang, so I was very embarrassed.

"Sorry to ring you at work, Hilary," he said when I told him how inconvenient it was, "but it's an emergency."

He told me that he and Ken, another of our friends, were supposed to be going to the pictures on a double date but one of the girls had let them down and he hoped I would please make the numbers up.

"We're not going out anymore," I reminded him curtly.

"It's not for me. It's for Ken."

And like a mug I agreed, although I did feel that he had a tremendous cheek to ask me. I think I only went because Ken was a very good friend of mine and I had spent a lot of time at his house with him and his family. I was very fond of him and loved his two little sisters. He was about a year younger than me, but we had a lot of shared interests. The two of us had spent a lot of time dancing together in his mother's kitchen to our favourite reggae records before I had started going out with James.

His mother loved me and made it clear she wanted me to be her future daughter-in-law. I loved her back, but I didn't love Ken in that way.

Anyway, the four of us did go to the cinema that weekend, and I was very surprised to see that James's new girlfriend looked just like me!

It was a very boring, supposedly funny war film rated an 18, and we all felt very daring as we were only 16 and 17 at the time.

Ken and I sat side by side throughout the film and he put his arm dutifully round me. It felt nice and warm but not romantic. Ken was just a good friend.

Afterwards, James went off in one direction to take his new girlfriend home, and Ken and I went the other way to the station so he could take me home on the train. He spent the whole journey with his arm around me again, and we kissed and cuddled for the twenty minutes of travelling. We did that because it's what you do on a date when you're 16 and 17. But it didn't feel right. Ken was a mate, not a boyfriend. His mother's wish for me as a daughter-in-law was never going to happen, and that evening was never mentioned again between Ken and me. We remain good friends even to this day.

After that, a few more boyfriends came and went, but nothing close or meaningful, and nothing lasting. I went out with any boy who asked. But those numbered very few. Fortunate really, considering the foolishness of such a way to carry on. I only did this because of my lack of confidence in myself and because of a vow that I had made at the age of about 13. For all my family must have loved me, I wasn't very happy at home and always felt second best to my sister. Because of this, I longed for a time when I would have a special someone who would really love me for myself. The little girl's dream of being loved, getting married, and having a family was very strong, so thinking that no one could possibly love me, the vow I had made to myself was that I would marry the first person who said that he loved me. It wouldn't matter if I didn't love him. I thought that someone who really loved me would look after me so well and be so nice to me that he would make me really happy. I also thought that if he was so good to me, eventually I would probably love him back, and that would be even better.

CHAPTER 8

Hannah Gets Married

SOMEHOW, THE BOYS I LIKED never liked me back. Once, when I was about 13, I dreamt that I had married George Harrison of the Beatles pop group. I dreamt that we had bought the beautiful manor house, Hall Place, where I went to school, and it was to be our home. We'd even installed a swimming pool in the grounds. It was such a good dream, I can remember it still, and I was quite sorry to wake up. I thought maybe it could be an omen and one day would come true. But fashion model Patti Boyd beat me to it before I was even out of socks.

I don't know if Hannah ever had dreams or fantasies as I had. I couldn't imagine that she did. She was far too sensible, but I found out something years later that I thought was rather sad. Apparently, a lovely young man who had worked for the same company as me had taken a liking to Hannah, but when he asked her out, she refused, even though she did like him. She was too frightened to ask permission from our mother.

When we were older, Hannah used to say to me that I was lucky to have been allowed to go out with boys as she never had been. But I think the truth of it was she was too scared to ask. She must've had other admirers. She was a very pretty and good-natured girl.

I never knew her to have any boyfriends until she was about 19 and started seeing a young man in secret. He was a work colleague of hers and of Indian origin. I knew and was sworn to secrecy, but eventually, our parents found out. Our mother was fury personified. Partly because of the deception, but mainly because he did not share our Christian beliefs. Our father was also disappointed and angry, but for a different reason. He wasn't interested in religion but was extremely colour prejudiced, which sadly was the general trend in our area at that time.

Things became more difficult for Hannah once the courtship was out in the open. She was not allowed to bring him home, and gradually she found she could not cope with the overbearing disapproval, particularly from our mother.

When it all became too much for her, she moved away from home and into a bedsit in London in the highly fashionable Hampstead Heath area.

I was very upset at my parents' disapproval as I wanted to see Hannah happy, and I was even more upset when she left home. My mother forbade me to visit her in London, and I missed her dreadfully.

After some months, we received a wedding invitation from Ron (his anglicised name) and Hannah. I was very excited. I wished with all my heart that I could be a bridesmaid, but there was no mention of that.

However, our mother made it clear that we would not be going. "How can we condone such an unchristian wedding?"

I was devastated. That was my sister. My only sister. And I wanted to see her happy on her big day.

Strangely enough, our mother made a condition. The condition was that if our father, as "head of the house", told us that we had to go, then we would go. Not that he ever "told" us we had to do anything. That seemed to be our mother's prerogative, but I lived the next few weeks in hope. Unfortunately, the chances were that his prejudices would prevent him from going anyway.

When the day of the wedding arrived, surprisingly, our father got up early and got dressed in his best suit. This was very unusual for a Saturday, which was usually his gardening day. He said nothing to us, but in expectation, we too put on our best clothes. I wanted to rush up to him and shout, "Please tell Mummy and me we have to go!" But I wouldn't dare. If our mother heard me, she would have accused me of condoning the unchristian union. Also, such excitable outbursts were unacceptable to our mother and classed as an ungodly lack of self-control.

All the time my father was getting ready, he never said a single word to us. In the end, he opened the front door and walked out, leaving us standing, still in our best clothes, waiting for an instruction that never came.

The door closed. We still stood there all dressed up. It was one of the only times I have seen my mother look close to tears. How I wished that my father had been a real "head of the house" that day. But I don't think it would ever have occurred to him to tell my strong-willed mother what to do.

"Come on," my mother said. "We can't stay here in our best clothes and be miserable. Let's go out."

So we climbed into the old Ford Prefect car that had replaced her Lambretta and drove off to Gravesend, to the home of my friend Ken and his dear mum and dad. I had got very close to his mother, Annette, who was now also my mother's friend.

Annette and her husband welcomed us in and made a big fuss of us both, which was much needed, although no consolation for missing my sister's wedding.

Before we left Annette, she took us upstairs and showed us her jewellery. She had a box full of silver and gold and made us laugh when she said she liked to sit up in bed at night polishing it. It was relaxing and therapeutic, she told us.

"Don't you do that?" she asked, grinning.

We looked at her blankly.

"Ain't you got no gold or silver?" Annette questioned in her down-to-earth manner.

It was obvious that neither of us had, although I would expect my mother's engagement and wedding rings had some value.

"Ya can't go through life wiv no gold or silver. 'Ere, you take these home." She sorted out a tiny, linked, gold chain for my mother, which she accepted graciously, and a lovely silver chain for me.

I was overwhelmed. I kissed and hugged my friend in thanks. I'd never had anything real silver before. I put it around my neck, and it's been there ever since. I treasure it more than I treasure any other material possessions. It stays round my neck every minute of the day as well as when I sleep and bath, and it's still the only thing I've ever owned that's real silver. The treasure is not so much the material worth as the sentimental value—that someone should want to give something of worth to me, Hilary.

I was sorry to say goodbye to dear Annette and her family. That night I cried myself to sleep with a mixture of emotions. I knew that I had missed one of the most important days of anyone's life and could never turn the clock back. I wondered how my father had got on that day and if he'd given my sister and her new husband a card or a present. I thought too about Annette and how kind she had been and eventually fell asleep with my hand clasping the silver chain around my neck.

Hannah and Ron's married life started off in a small bedsit that I was able to visit, but only after I myself had left home. They showed me their wedding photos. Hannah looked beautiful. She wore a white lace minidress with a long, white veil. But what caught my eye particularly was the picture of Hannah and Ron signing the register, Hannah with her hand poised holding the pen and looking down at the paper. Her eye make-up was immaculate, extremely 1960s with the pale eyeshadow smudged smoothly over her lids, a thick black line outlining the crease, and long, long black eyelashes sweeping down towards her pale cheeks. As soon as I saw that photo, I decided that if and when I got married, that's exactly how I'd have my make-up and have a photo taken of me looking down and signing the register.

Ron looked very debonaire in the photos in his smart suit and neatly groomed hair. A very handsome young man, and his dark features complimented my blonde sister's.

Another photo that stays in my mind is one that was taken outside the Hampstead Heath registry office. There are my sister looking wonderful and Ron in his smart suit, and proudly standing beside Hannah is my father.

After the wedding, the couple went to one of the Channel Islands for their honeymoon. I must admit I envied them. I wondered if I would ever meet someone who would want to marry me, and I could have my make-up just so for the signing of the register and have a honeymoon in some exotic place like the Channel Islands.

Hannah and Ron eventually moved from their tiny bedsit into a quaint little house just outside London. Later, they moved to a bigger house elsewhere, and later still, they moved to an even bigger and better house in the stockbroker belt of Wokingham. All this time, Ron was working hard and climbing the executive ladder, so they had moved house to go with the job. I believe his name was even on some of the company's headed notepaper. He must've reached the top! Hannah had, and still has, every reason to be proud of him, even though he has now taken early retirement. I think the next step up the ladder would have been to move abroad, which neither of them wanted to do.

I've always felt proud of both of them for more reasons than I can count, but mainly just because she's my big sister.

From the day they got married to the best of my knowledge, my sister has had a very happy marriage to Ron, and over the years, both my mother and father came to accept Ron as part of the family at last.

CHAPTER 9

Independence

I REALLY MISSED HANNAH ONCE she had left home. I did manage to see her a few times after she was married though because I left home at 18 myself and could go where I pleased with no reprisals.

It was around this time that I decided I hated my name and would shorten it to Helen. I was no longer the schoolgirl Hilary that no one would touch because of the lurgy, and I was no longer the teenage thief who had to be ostracised. My family said, "How on earth could Hilary be shortened to Helen?" "Because it just can," I told them. And from then on, except to my family, I became Helen.

For the first few weeks of my newfound independence, I stayed with a sweet, elderly lady who gave me a room and meals. I had moved to North London to do some voluntary work with the Bible group, and the society had organised for me to stay with Ruth, an elderly spinster, until I got on my feet.

When I first arrived at her house, Ruth very sweetly offered me a cup of tea. As children, all we'd drank was milk, water, or squash, and only when I had started my working life at Ash Tapes did I discover my taste for coffee. I refused the tea but was too shy to ask for a cup of coffee instead, and Ruth then offered me a cup of Horlicks. I'd only ever had Horlicks at bedtime, but I felt that it was the better option and said, "Yes, please." It did seem very odd though, drinking Horlicks in the middle of the day.

From then on, first thing in the morning, after all meals, and last thing at night, Ruth made me a big mug of Horlicks. Every day,

Horlicks. All day, Horlicks. And before the first week was over, I hated Horlicks. But I just couldn't tell her. After I moved away from Ruth's, I never drank Horlicks again.

The first thing I had to do when I arrived in London (apart from getting used to the Horlicks) was to find a part-time job to support myself. One lady in our Bible group there worked as a receptionist for a dentist who was looking for a part-time dental nurse. She introduced me, and although I had no previous experience in that field, I got the job and would be trained as I went. The receptionist, Hilda, was very sweet. She was the mother of Brian Bennett of the Shadows, who at that time were the backing group for Cliff Richard. I did meet Brian and his family a couple of times so this was my big boast and claim to contacts with the rich and famous during my stay in London.

At the dental surgery, the staff were all very friendly and I made friends in particular with one of the other young dental nurses. At lunchtimes, we would go off together to the local cafes, where she introduced me to pie and mash and spaghetti bolognaise.

Dental nursing was not my best idea of a job though. I saw some pretty ghastly things during the time I was employed there. One poor patient had her jaw accidentally broken while having a wisdom tooth removed. Her husband was called in, and he promptly passed out on the floor! We had to organise a taxi to take her to the local hospital to have her jaw wired up. The poor husband was in such a state that I was instructed to go in the taxi with them. Also, her husband, being Turkish, didn't speak English well enough to know exactly what was going on, and of course, his wife was unable to say anything at all. It turned out that the poor man was more concerned as to who would cook his dinner than how his injured wife would fare.

Another thing that always turned my stomach was watching patients having root treatment and the stitching up of the gum afterwards. It looked to me just about the most painful treatment anyone could have, and thankfully it's a treatment that so far I've never had to undergo.

There were two dentists working at the surgery. Unfortunately, the dentist I worked with was not very hot on hygiene. He would have his coffee break, eat a roll, and smoke a cigarette, then go back to work without even washing his hands. In those days, they didn't wear surgical gloves either. Worse still, sometimes he would even pick his nose.

I did once witness someone die in the dentist's chair. We had the anaesthetist there at the time and I think the patient may have had a heart problem that had not been recorded on his notes.

After I'd got my job, I moved out of Ruth's house and into a rented room. I went to an address after reading an advertisement in a shop window, and as I approached the house to enquire, I saw that it stood out from the rest of the street with its brightly coloured brickwork. I felt puzzled by this as I walked up to the front door, but on the other side of the door was a lovely, friendly Greek family. I discovered later that this gaudy appearance was very typical of the Greek families' houses in that area. Or in any area, most probably.

The husband invited me in straight away and showed me the room they were wanting to rent out. It was a small, south-facing bedroom with a window overlooking their tiny backyard. The room consisted of a single bed, a wardrobe, and a sideboard. I thought the room would be no good because I needed some cooking facilities, but the husband was only too eager to put that right. He said he would buy a little stove of some sort that I could have in the room.

One week later I moved in, and true to his word, my new landlord had put two new electric cooking rings in my room.

They made me very welcome with their generous hospitality. I noticed that the husband, George, did all the talking. This was because his wife, Genna, could not speak any English. They had a dear little girl, Rebee, who was 5 years old. She could speak both languages so through her, I was able to communicate with Genna.

The day I moved in, George invited me back downstairs to have a cup of coffee with them. (No more Horlicks for me now.)

"Oh yes, please. I love coffee!" I responded, a bit too eagerly.

"We'll have lunch first," said George, and Genna came in from the kitchen with a big, glass bowl full of various salad stuff tossed in oil. It was very tasty and quite different from the basic salads I was used to. With it, we ate some homemade herb bread followed by yoghurt for dessert.

After we'd finished our meal, Genna brought in a tray of the originally offered coffee. *What tiny cups*, was my first thought, which I kept to myself. Also no milk. I thought perhaps Genna would go back in the kitchen for some, but I soon saw that it was their custom to drink it without.

Not wanting to appear awkward or rude, I decided to do the same. My first mouthful told me this was some seriously strong coffee. After having enthused about my love of coffee, I felt obliged to drink it all without any negative comment, but it was certainly not like any coffee I'd had before. It had a bitter and distinctive nutty flavour, and the last mouthful completely filled my mouth with a mass of tiny grouts. It was a shock, and it was as much as I could do not to choke and splutter loudly. I found out soon enough that this was Turkish coffee, and although free at last of the dreaded Horlicks, now I had to suffer a small cup of strong, bitter Turkish coffee every day. I soon learnt to leave the last few mouthfuls in the bottom of the cup!

A couple of weeks after I'd moved in, there was a light tap on my bedroom door. I opened it to find George, Genna, and little Rebee standing there. Rebee was clasping a small, round fishbowl in her plump hands.

"We didn't want you to be lonely," George said, Genna smiling behind him, "so we've brought the goldfish up for you."

How thoughtful. The bowl, the goldfish, and even a tub of fish food. George explained how much and how often to feed the fish and assured me that I could keep Oscar in my room for as long as I lived there.

In the months that I was there, I never built up any kind of rapport with Oscar, but I fed him regularly as instructed and I never killed him off, so I guess that was OK. And I had to admit they were a sweet family to make such a well-meaning gesture.

Another afternoon, George knocked on my door after work. "This is for you." He held out a box that I took with thanks.

I thought it was an Easter egg, but when I opened the box, I found that it was a large tub of ice cream. In all my time there, George and Genna were very good to me, and little Rebee was a delight.

I made two really good friends during my time in London. One was Sandra, who was a bit younger than me. Her mother was an invalid so she had to do all the chores, including the shopping, which is where we had a lot of fun together. I had to shop for myself anyway, so we would go together, and in the butchers we used, the young lads there used to try to flirt with us. We weren't interested, so we pretended we were both married ladies and talked loudly about what chops or sausages our husbands would like for tea!

One Sunday after the Bible meeting, Sandra and I had planned on going for a picnic to Alexandra Palace, and we had our sandwiches with us ready to go. Before we left the hall, a young man named Nick, who we knew rather liked Sandra, asked her out to the cinema that afternoon. She said no because she and I were going on a picnic. So he kindly said, "Why don't you both come to the pictures with me then?"

So we did. I'm not sure that he really wanted me there as well, but he offered so I went. We saw *Chitty Chitty Bang Bang* together. During the film, the family on the screen started having a picnic, which reminded us of our sandwiches in our bags, so we got them out and started munching them either side of him. He was a bit prim and proper and was so embarrassed that he left his seat and didn't come back until we'd finished! After the film, Sandra and I giggled so much about it, and about the film in general, that it put him off and he never asked her out again. I don't think she was overly bothered.

My other friend was Arianne. She was a few years older than me and had a dear, little girl called Sophie. Arianne was a single parent, so little Sophie came everywhere with us. I remember once going to a fun fair with them and we wanted to go on the Big Wheel, so Sophie had to sit in the middle of us. She screamed the whole of the ride! And she still remembers it now. No "health and safety" in those days!

I stuck at the dental nursing job for as long as I lived in London. It kept me busy two days a week, and the wages just about paid my rent and kept me fed while I carried out my voluntary assignment for the rest of the week. A few years later, I read in my father's newspaper that the dentist I had worked with had been struck off for misconduct. I wasn't overly surprised.

CHAPTER 10

Meeting Jim

WELL, MY TIME OF INDEPENDENCE came to an end after about a year. I'd made a couple of really good girlfriends in Sandra and Arianne, and I've stayed in touch with them down to this day. I had to go into hospital to have my tonsils out. Not a major thing, but I gave up my room and my job and went back home to my parents so that I could recuperate there.

The tonsillectomy went smoothly, and once I was fit for work again, I was fortunate enough to get my old job back at Ash Tapes. The business had got bigger and there were a few more members of staff. My boss and his family had moved into a big house in the country, and the business had now extended throughout the whole of the large Victorian house where the top three floors used to be their living quarters. I did miss the little girls though.

Now that I was older, I had a little bit more freedom. I missed my sister who was married and living and working in London still. She didn't come to visit us because of our parents' antagonism, but while I had lived away, I had managed a few sneaky visits that fortunately never got found out. One time she had cooked sausages for dinner—my absolute favourite—and the story goes that I ate a whole pound of them all by myself. I don't really remember, but it's very likely true, and they're still my favourites. Hannah still cooks them for me when I visit.

Another time, they claimed that I turned up on the arm of some young, hippy lad that I'd met on the train there that day. I don't remember that either. I've never been sure if they're pulling my leg or if I've blanked it out in embarrassment.

What I do remember on one visit was her Indian husband making the most delicious curry I had ever tasted. And what amazed me about it was that he never used a single scrap of curry powder! He had used various different spices that I'd never heard of before, so I had my first truly authentic Indian curry, something that was practically unheard of back then before Indian takeaways started appearing on the high streets.

So once back home again, it was good to see my old friends from the Bible group and catch up on all their news. We started going up to London every couple of weeks for an evening's ice skating. One of the lads owned a little van, so one lucky mate (usually one of the girls he had his eye on) got to sit up front with him while the rest of us sat on the floor in the back of the van in the dark. No seatbelts back then. We rolled about as we drove round corners, and a lot of giggling went on.

Some weeks we went bowling instead. That was much more local, but for me, the ice rink held all the magic. There were amazing disco lights changing colour over the rink and loud music playing to add to the atmosphere. Sometimes a disc jockey would be there, but often they had a live pop band so we'd skate round to the front of the stage to ogle at them! I could think of no better place to spend an evening than in this wonderful musical, magical fairyland with the exhilarating feeling as you zoomed along at top speed or sailed around the ice in a dream.

Around that time, I met a young man who lived quite close to me, and joy of joys, he asked me out. I leapt at that! He was a nice-looking lad and quite genteel. I thought I would like to get to know him better. Fortunately, he was attached to the same Bible group, although in the next town. And wonder of wonders, my mother seemed to like him, even to the extent of making a joke before he picked me up for our first date. He had a little moustache and she said, much to my surprise, "That won't half tickle!"

Well, he came, and off we went on the bus to the cinema. He knew the bus conductor so we were let off from paying our fare. I forget now what the film was, but we certainly behaved ourselves. Then he brought me home, made another arrangement to see me, and gave me a little peck on the cheek.

So when I went indoors, what did I do? In my sheer joy of what I thought would be the start of something good, I said to my mother, "You were right. It did tickle!"

Oh, she was just horrified! "You didn't let him kiss you on your first date, did you?"

Boy, was I in trouble. Also, I stupidly told her that we had got free bus travel because he knew the conductor, and I got well and truly scolded for that too. It was dishonest, she said. Maybe it was, but she never seemed to approve of anything anyway.

The relationship with this young man didn't go anywhere after all. We just went out two or three times more, and the last time, we went to a friend's house for what we called a record session, with all our favourite songs from the charts. There were about half a dozen of us, and he spent the entire evening sitting on the lap of a very large, jolly, fat girl, the life and soul of the party type of girl. This girl has actually remained a good friend of mine until her sad death a few years ago. But although this boy never actually dated our mutual friend, it was my last date with him. I took his behaviour as a large hint and was very disappointed.

Later this same year, I had another brief friendship with a young man. He wasn't part of our Bible group so I had to keep it a secret. He was about ten years older than me and the brother of someone we knew from the group. That is how I came to meet him. He was blond and very handsome but also very troubled. I must have been a sucker for an underdog as I thought I could make him happy. I realise now that a lot of his troubles he had brought on himself, but at that time, I was very naïve and was flattered by the attention of someone so much older and seemingly more mature. We didn't go on any proper dates apart from a visit to a travelling funfair, but I would occasionally meet him for a kiss and a cuddle at the end of the day, when he'd finished work on a nearby building site. Oh, how I could just live off hugs and cuddles!

Once when my parents were away camping, he came round to my home late one evening. I was warming some tomato soup on the stove for my supper at the time. He came in for a little while, and we did a lot of kissing and cuddling. I could smell the soup and really looked forward to ending the evening, after the cuddles, with my bowl of soup before going to bed.

He took his leave after about twenty minutes, leaving me happy, rather giddy, and anticipating my supper. When I went into the kitchen, the soup was gently simmering away in the pan, and there, lying right in the middle of it, was a huge, great, dead bluebottle! No supper for me after all.

Shortly after this, the friendship ended. His sister had found out and warned him off. She also warned me, in a very kindly way, that he was really bad news and explained the reasons why. She also promised not to tell my mother, a promise that she thankfully kept.

Back to the ice skating. I was loving it still. There was an added bonus too. It was a known fact that lots of the youngsters from the same Bible groups from surrounding areas all went skating there on the particular Sundays that we went. In fact, it was known by many back then as the Bible groups' dating ground! I don't think my mother could have known this, or I would never have been allowed to go.

One evening at the ice rink, a young man I didn't know took my hand to skate round with him. Unfortunately, I couldn't understand a word he was saying at first. After two or three times around the rink with him, I realised that he wasn't from any of our friends' groups and he was talking in rather a coarse way, so I made my excuses and came off the ice. I realised now that the first thing he'd actually said to me was "I'm Irish," to which I'd replied, "I'm Helen." The same evening, not long after that, another young man, Chris, asked to take me round on the ice, and that was a much better experience. By the end of the evening, he had asked me out, so I was very happy about that.

Chris was a very nice lad and we went out together for a while, but the relationship was never going to go anywhere. We didn't seem to have any chemistry between us, and much as I'm ashamed to say this now, he was rather boring.

Shortly before we split up, we went for a day out to Camber Sands with a whole lot of his mates. First, he picked me up in his car then drove me back to Penge where there was a convoy of cars waiting for everyone to arrive before setting off.

"I'm taking my best friend and his girlfriend too," Chris told me as a lanky, young man in a funny seaside hat bounded up to the car, followed by a pretty girl with several bags and a rucksack. They got in, and I was introduced to Jim and Anna. Straight away, I liked Jim. He looked so happy and full of fun and was making us all laugh during the drive to the coast.

It was lovely at the beach with golden sands and plenty of sunshine, with lots of laughing and joking with new friends. One of the lads had brought a portable record player along with a pile of records, so we had music on the beach. Quite a novelty back then.

Jim's girlfriend, Anna, was incredibly organised. She'd brought absolutely everything that could possibly be needed for a day out at the beach. She spread out a tablecloth at lunchtime and then produced lots of Tupperware pots containing sandwiches, sausage rolls, cakes, and biscuits, and other food. Enough to feed our car party, which was good, because it hadn't occurred to me to bring a packed lunch.

When everyone went in swimming, I declined. I hadn't brought my costume anyway, as well as being very shy about showing a bit of flesh in front of anyone. Jim said he wasn't going in either, so the two of us stayed on the beach and got to know each other. He was really funny, which appealed to me, my own family being much more serious and practical minded.

By the time everyone came out of the water, we were laughing together like old friends, and best of all, I was wearing his hat.

CHAPTER 11

Courtship and Marriage

IT WASN'T LONG AFTER THE Camber Sands trip that Chris and I split up, albeit amicably, and in a few weeks, he had started dating my friend Lisa. Through her, I discovered that Jim had also split up with his girlfriend, Anna.

Some smart thinking had to be done. I knew that Chris, Jim, and their mates would meet up on a Sunday afternoon for a friendly football game, and sometimes they took their girlfriends along to cheer them on. So I asked Lisa to please ask Chris if he would pick me up, along with her, the following Sunday. Unbeknown to me, Jim had also asked Chris to see if Lisa could get me to come along with them. This is what happened, and this is where our story as a couple begins.

After the boys' kick-about, our little crowd went back to Jim's parents' house as they lived nearby, and we had refreshments. It was nice to meet them straight away, but I was quite baffled. His mum, a little, round Geordie woman with a gruff voice and strong accent, seemed to be shouting, "Raif!" "Rex!" "Rex!" "Raif!" "Rex!" several times over, and I couldn't fathom out who was Rex and who was Raif! Jim put me straight on that. His dad and his brother were both called Raif, and the dog was Rex. Things made a lot more sense after I got that sorted.

From then on, we were a couple, and I really enjoyed his company. He was so funny and easy-going, always with a joke or a wisecrack. He never failed to make me laugh. Sometimes he would surprise me by doing things or taking me places on the spur of the moment, so very different from my own forward-thinking family. I think this was a lot of the appeal, his completely different outlook on life.

He had a blue Vespa scooter, and I just loved to ride pillion with him, never knowing where we might be going. Sometimes it was to visit mates, and sometimes to show me his childhood haunts. If he'd been to the barbers before he picked me up, I would be sniffing his hair while we rode along. Whatever his barber had used on his hair, I just couldn't get enough of it!

I gradually learned all about his background. But I'm here to tell my story, not his, so I'll just give a potted version of it.

When he was just 6 months old, his parents fell on hard times, and Jim and his older brother and sister all went into a children's home. They promised not to split the siblings up, but sadly they didn't stick to their word. Jim spent most of his childhood in the children's home, while his brother and sister were fostered out. At age 16, he left the children's home and joined the army's Junior Leaders. He was there for about a year, and when he came out, he lived in a hostel. He told me he'd always felt like he was just a number—in the home, the army, and the hostel. This made me feel so sad. I wanted more than ever to make him feel special, wanted, and cared about. About a year before I'd met him, he and his brother and sister, both of whom were already married, had managed to trace their parents, who welcomed them in, but sadly, none of them had a close bond with them due to circumstances. From then on, Jim lived with them.

Over the weeks, our courtship went from strength to strength, while Chris and Lisa didn't stay a couple. Jim's parents seemed to like me and always made a big fuss of me. They were very different from my own family. They were quite rough and ready and always very hard up, but they had kind hearts, I thought.

On the other hand, my parents didn't take to Jim at all. They tried to warn me off him, saying they could see he was a bad lot. But that just made me draw closer to him, to prove them wrong. It was true though that he'd had a variety of jobs. Some for very short periods of time. But I just thought he was "damaged goods" and wanted to help him.

One day my parents said they'd had a letter from his mum and dad, saying how dishonest he'd been—and worse. But they wouldn't show me the letter. I was very upset because I didn't think my parents would make something like that up. But on the other hand, why on earth would his parents write it? What did they write, and what was the "worse"?

After a few months, my father said I had to stop seeing him. But he said if he could get a job and keep it for six months, then we could get back together.

Would I be a nice, obedient daughter? No. I felt Jim really needed me. So after about a month of no contact, I left home with a bag of belongings and went off to his parents' house.

When I arrived, they welcomed me in and told me Jim had just gone to the shop for them and wouldn't be long. When we heard his key in the door, they said, "Quick, hide. Let's surprise him."

So I dutifully crouched behind the settee.

"Jimmy, we've got a surprise for you," his dad said when he walked into the room.

His reply was "Have you bought me a drum kit?"

Oh dear. Did I really come second to a set of drums? They laughed, and I jumped out from the settee to hug him.

I was shocked though. He looked so different. Scruffy, spotty, the beginnings of a beard, and a cigarette dangling from his hand. I'd never known him to smoke. I'd also heard him casually swearing while acknowledging his parents when he'd come through the front door. Was this really the same Jim I'd been seeing the few months previously? Well, he had to be. I'd made my choice, and here I was. There was no going back now for me. I thought our being split up must have affected him really badly for him to have changed so much. But now we were back together, surely, he would go back to the real him, and I would wait for that.

I was given the third bedroom there, although we did spend some time in his room, and sometimes we did a Bible study together so I felt reassured that he still remembered the good values he used to live by and that he would get back to how he had been in time.

We weren't sticking rigidly to our beliefs now though. We took to taking Rex for long walks through the fields and took great advantage of this time alone there. Very often his parents would say, "How does

Rex get back so long before you?" We knew sex before marriage was against our Christian beliefs but felt that as we'd slept together, we were now married in God's eyes. All we needed to do to put this right was to make it legal.

One exciting thing about living with his parents was that they had a television. Our family had never owned one, so in the evenings, I was glued to it, along with his mum. We watched all the soaps, the shows, and the films. I couldn't get enough of it! Even *Top of the Pops* on a Thursday night.

Jim's dad was quite the joker. I remember the time he came home with a little, second-hand, old banger. The four of us had a few trips out in it before it fell to pieces. Once, not far from home, he stopped, wound his window down, and asked a passer-by if we were on the right road to Glasgow. We were in Bromley. Another time, he stuck marshmallows all over his face and drove the entire time like that. When we got home, he ate them. They all loved their sweets, as did I. Often, early evening, we would take a walk across the fields to a little shack that sold cigarettes and sweets. I noticed that they all seemed to have a compulsion to spend every last penny, down to buying penny sweets, so that all the money was gone.

Over the weeks, Jim's crude language got worse, and he seemed to have a really bad temper, which I'd not previously witnessed. Also, his family seemed to shout and argue a lot of the time, as if this was normal for them, with all the effing and blinding flying round the room. How I hated that. But I was bound to him now so I had to accept all that went with the commitment.

After one huge row, we both walked out and they shouted, "Don't come back!" So we went to a nearby pub where the two of us used to go occasionally. At the end of the evening, after a couple of drinks and a game of darts, we headed to the local train station. Here, Jim had a friend who was a station porter, and as he was on duty that evening, he let us sleep in his little porters' hut at the end of the station. In the morning, I got up and had a wash and brush-up in the station's ladies' room. I was still working at Ash Tapes so I had to get an early bus to work.

We spent the next few nights in the porters' hut, but it was very cold and uncomfortable. I also realised now that I might be pregnant.

Birth control? I had no idea about it back then. All our mother taught us was abstinence and something odd about a man's bits feeling like an orange. I had no idea what she was talking about back then. The next night when we went to the porters' hut, it was all locked up and his mate was off duty, so we walked a couple of miles to where he knew there were trains waiting in the sidings for the night. We climbed over a fence and scrambled down a steep slope to the railway tracks. Then we climbed into one of the trains and slept there. That was even more cold and uncomfortable than the porters' hut. We did this for several weeks, again, me freshening up in the platform ladies' before I headed to work each day. We did occasionally go back to the comparative luxury of the porters' hut when his mate was back on night duty.

When it was my payday or his dole money day, we would go to the local pub in the evening. One evening, when we left to go to our train for the night, one of Jim's mates said he'd had a row with his mum so he'd come with us. After the long walk, when we got to the fence and climbed over, he took one look at the slope and said, "I'm not climbing down that!" And he went back home.

After a few weeks of living like that, Jim got a live-in job at the pub as a bar and cellarman, and I got some lodgings with a friend from the pub. On the odd occasion, Jim would sneak me upstairs to his room and we'd share his single bed. But he wouldn't come up until the early hours of the morning and wouldn't tell me what he'd been doing all that time. Presumably drinking downstairs. He was drinking and swearing a lot now and could be quite nasty to me too. I kept telling myself, "He will go back to being the real him when things get better for us."

One evening, when it was snowing, I went back to my lodgings and found I was locked out. I knocked for a long time and even sat on the doorstep for ages, thinking my landlady would come back at some point and let me in. In the end, I went back to the pub, which was now all locked up for the night, so I threw some pebbles at Jim's bedroom window. But to no avail. In the end, I curled up on the back doorstep and shivered and cried for a long time before I fell asleep there in the snow.

The two of us started spending some time with my landlady, Angie, and her boyfriend. I quite liked the idea of having some friends, as we weren't in touch with any of our old pals now. Mostly it was just evenings at the pub where Jim was working. One day, because we never had any money, Angie said she'd take us shopping. Before we got to the shops, she showed us the inside of her coat that was totally lined with large pockets, as was her boyfriend's. I couldn't believe how much stuff they came out of the shop with. I'd just bought a mascara but was a bit suspicious of what Jim came out with, knowing he had no money. I was quite shocked as this thieving seemed to be normal to them. In fact, it upset me so much that I decided I didn't want to lodge there anymore. They thought I was very odd and all laughed at me, even Jim.

Once I'd given up my room at Angie's, Jim would sneak me back up to his little room in the pub every night. But again, he wouldn't come up until the early hours of the morning. He'd obviously been drinking a lot and behaved rather oddly. More than once, he'd put his hands around my throat, and I'd wake up in shock, fighting him off. Then he'd say sorry and be mumbling stuff that I couldn't understand. After all that, we didn't get to sleep until about five or six in the morning.

When I asked Jim the next morning why he'd been attacking me, he'd deny any knowledge of it and claim it must be the drink. It didn't stop him from drinking though. One night I remember a huge blow to the back of my head. The next thing I knew was that we were at the open window and he was trying to push me out. After a struggle, he stopped and tried to jump out himself. It took all my strength to stop him. Again, in the morning, he denied all knowledge of it. In the end, I had to give up my job at Ash Tapes as I was just too tired to function there.

Then came another blow. He lost his job and digs at the pub. When I asked why, he was very vague, saying there was a misunderstanding about some money. I felt very worried as I remembered that some months previously he'd lost his job as a milkman, supposedly because of a "misunderstanding about some money". I didn't want to think badly of him, but to happen twice? It did bother me, but if I asked any questions, he'd just yell at me. My father's doubts loomed back at me.

With no money between us now, we went back to his parents with our tails between our legs, and thankfully, they took us back in. His mum was really excited to know I was pregnant, and Jim and I went and booked our wedding. We still had to have our separate rooms though, and we still took Rex for his walks. We even went back to having our Bible discussions in his room sometimes. I felt things could only get better now.

One afternoon, Jim went to his bedroom and was gone for a long time. After a while, I went up to see what he was doing and found his door locked. "Go away!" he shouted.

"Why? What's the matter?" I asked.

"Just go away" came from in the room. I felt worried and had a bad feeling inside, so I kept knocking. In the end, he opened his door the smallest crack he could and peeped out. What I saw really shocked me. He had a face full of make-up. For a brief moment, I thought he was his sister, as they were very alike. I could see through the crack that he was wearing a dress and high heels as well.

"*Why?*" I asked.

He said he loved me so much that he wanted to see what it felt like to be me. I just could not get my head around this. It was something completely alien to me, and I didn't like it. I went back downstairs, and in a short while, he followed me down, looking like his usual self again. It was never mentioned again.

For my upcoming wedding, I bought a very pretty, purple, knee-length dress with a silver panel down the front, which I'd found in a little, tucked-away boutique. I also bought some white shoes and a big, white, floppy hat to wear. Jim's mum bought a big, blue, floppy hat too. A few invitations were sent, just to family. It would be a small affair at the local registry office.

When the day came, we'd already been arguing with his mum because I wanted to arrange the vases of flowers in the living room where the small reception would be. But she insisted on doing it and taking over practically everything else. It seemed like it was her day, not mine.

I had a pretty bouquet of purple and white freesias, and the men had a flower in their buttonholes. Jim's brother Raif was due to pick us all up in his car, but when he didn't turn up, Jim and I, along with his parents, all set off in our wedding finery to catch the bus. Jim looked so smart. He'd got a new suit, shoes, and all the trimmings from Burton on a credit plan. Before we reached the bus stop, we spotted a black cab coming towards us and hailed it down. At least we would arrive in style after all.

I couldn't wait to become Helen Jones. I thought it had a much better ring to it than Hilary Thrift. I thought too about how straight after the ceremony Jim and I would go off together as husband and wife. We were just a small group there. His brother arrived late with his wife, Brenda, and their little girl, full of apologies, and his uncle and aunt and their children were there, and Jim's mate the railway porter was there, as well as Jim's parents of course. None of my family came.

After the wedding, I grabbed my new husband's hand ready to go back to the house for the reception. But his dad and uncle grabbed his other arm and announced that the menfolk were all going to the pub for a bit while the ladies and children went back to the house. I wanted to cry. He was my brand-new husband and they'd snatched him away from me.

Back at the house, another argument ensued over the preparation of the refreshments. Clearly, I wasn't getting a say in anything. My mother-in-law organised everything. She being a good cook had made the base of our wedding cake and iced it. Brenda worked in a bakery, and she had brought the top layer from there, complete with some decorations on top, including little bride and groom figures. Also, she'd brought the four pillars to put the two cakes together. However, when we went to assemble the cake, we discovered that our top tier with all its decorations was actually bigger than the bottom, homemade one. I was worried that there'd be another row, but in fact, everybody laughed. We just swapped the cakes and took the decorations off the one and put them on the other. Nobody would have guessed!

When the men finally came back, there were all very tipsy. Rude jokes were flying about, and there was a lot of crude talk, which I felt very embarrassed about. At one point during the evening, the lights fused. There was a lot of hilarity about that, along with Jim's cousin being shut in a cupboard. It wasn't like any reception or party I'd been to before. All the men were completely drunk at the end of it, including Jim, whose coarse mouth and dirty jokes at my expense really upset me. We'd received just one present, a baby layette set that his parents bought us, ready for when our baby arrived in a few months.

CHAPTER 12

Peterborough

IT WAS A VERY DIFFICULT time living with my new in-laws. Jim seemed to be their skivvy, running errands for them all the time, going back and forth to the shop several times a day, and to the betting office for his dad. None of us was working so money was very tight, which caused a lot of anxiety.

After two weeks of marriage, there was a knock on the door. Next thing I knew, Jim was carted off to prison for three weeks for non-payment of fines. I had no idea what the fines had been for, and of course, there was nothing I could do about it if I had known. Not a good start to our married life.

The three weeks went by, then we got on with our life together. Sadly, he came out of prison with even more swearing, crudity, and cursing than before he went in. Every week, there were rows between him and his parents. I just tried to keep out of it, but eventually, the rows and yelling got so bad every day that we decided to leave again.

His brother Raif had moved to Peterborough to work and had rented a brand-new house for his little family on the work scheme, so we decided to go and join them and see if we could get a house too. We packed our few possessions up and loaded them on the second-hand pram we'd bought for when our baby came and set off.

When we got to London, we had quite a walk to the station that we needed. We must have looked an odd sight, with me pregnant and Jim pushing the loaded pram. On our way, we came to a road packed with people, including war veterans in their attire. We then realised it was

Armistice Day. They were holding the two-minute silence, but we just trudged past them with our pram, probably looking like Steptoe and Wife. We just wanted to get on our way to our new life.

It was a long journey from London to Peterborough on the train, and when we finally got there, we made our way to Raif and Brenda's house. They were most surprised to see us, along with our loaded pram, but fortunately, they welcomed us in. They didn't seem to mind that we'd plonked ourselves unexpectedly on them, and they both agreed that they wouldn't want to live with the parents either.

The next day, Jim went to work with his brother to see if he could get a job and a house on the same scheme, but unfortunately, that scheme had finished, although he did get some work there. So we lodged with Raif and Brenda for a while. They had a dear little girl with pretty, blonde curls. She was about 2 years old, and Brenda was expecting another baby, due shortly after mine. By this time, I only had about six weeks to go, but at least Brenda and I had something in common as I hardly knew her before then.

While we were staying there, Jim and I had our own little silly joke about calling our baby Armitage Shanks. That was because every time we used the toilet there, our eyes were on a level with the maker's name on the sink, which was Armitage Shanks. In fact, we started referring to our unborn baby as Armitage. Raif and Brenda thought we were bonkers!

One day, the police called there, looking for Jim. No one would tell me what it was about, and the upshot was that he had to go to court. I was completely in the dark about it all. Raif just said, "You don't want to know." But I did. Though I never found out what it was all about.

About four weeks before "Armitage" was due, we moved a few miles away to a caravan park and rented one of them. At last, for the first time, we had a little place of our own. It wasn't easy. We had to go outside to collect our water, and for the toilets, whatever the weather.

Because of his mysterious court business, Jim now had a social worker who would occasionally visit us. He was very kind, and sometimes he brought little things for the baby and even some bits of jewellery for me. I didn't know anything about social workers or what their job entailed, but to me, this one seemed like a nice, posh, helpful uncle.

Jim soon lost his job with his brother. He told me it was over a misunderstanding and he hadn't done anything wrong. I'd heard that tale before. I did wonder if it had anything to do with the court business, but whatever the reason, it meant that we went back to being really skint.

When I went into labour, one of our caravan neighbours drove us to the hospital in his truck. There I gave birth to a tiny, dear, little girl. In those days, they kept new mothers in for ten days, as a matter of course, and during that time, we were helped with our breastfeeding and taught how to bath and top and tail our babies as well as how to put on the terry-towelling nappies. No disposable ones in those days. This was all very useful because I'd had no experience of looking after little babies. We called our daughter Melissa. All the nurses loved her and nicknamed her Rosebud.

The other new mums on the ward had loads of congratulations cards, balloons, gifts, and flowers that I admired, wishing I had some too. But as always, Jim was skint so no gifts or flowers for me. Maybe next time, I thought, as we had planned to have two children. I was also upset because we seemed to have left our lovely baby layette set behind at his parents' house.

Jim came with our neighbour to fetch me home from the hospital after the ten days, and Jim said there was a surprise waiting for me at home. Flowers? Balloons? I couldn't wait.

But as I walked up the steps to go in, I could hear a lot of chatter, and on entering our tiny living room, I was shocked to find about ten people all squashed in there, waiting to greet me. There were Raif and Brenda and their little girl, and the rest were our caravan neighbours, most of whom I didn't actually know. I went straight into the bedroom as Melissa needed a feed. I didn't want to go in there with them all laughing, telling dirty jokes, and drinking. I just wanted Jim to come into the bedroom to see if I was all right. But he didn't, so after about an hour, I went into the living room with them all, feeling like a fish out of water. After they'd all gone, Jim was really angry with me for not joining in. I wondered, *Just how well does he really know me?*

When Melissa was a couple of weeks old, I told Jim that I wanted to get back into our Bible group and wondered if there was one nearby. So one day, when we had walked into town with Melissa in her pram, we asked at the police station if they knew of one. They were very helpful and gave us the address and some directions. It took us nearly two hours to walk to the address, but when we arrived, it turned out to be a spiritualist hall. Definitely not what we were looking for! In fact, all the time we lived in Peterborough, we were never able to find the Bible group. I was upset at this because it was my one hope that by finding this wholesome group, I could finally get the "real" Jim back.

After about six weeks, I began to experience difficulties feeding my baby, so I gradually weaned her onto a bottle. She took to it well, but that wasn't without its difficulties.

First of all, we had to rely on Calor gas for our cooker, and occasionally it would run out just when I needed to boil the kettle to make the bottle. Then Jim would more than likely have to run around trying to borrow some money from his brother, or a neighbour, then buy a gas bottle and get it back and connected while a hungry Melissa screamed her head off.

Another problem lay with the matches. We always had a matchbox by the cooker to light it with, and Jim would always use the same matches for lighting his cigarettes. The problem was that he always put the dead matches back in the box. I kept asking him not to. When I went to bed, I would shake the box to make sure there were some matches in there so I could boil the kettle for Melissa's night feed. But I lost count of the times in the middle of the night when the matches in the box turned out all to be dead ones. I could never get Jim to wake up, so I had to go knocking on the neighbours' doors to scrounge a match, in the early hours of the morning.

We didn't have a washing machine in the caravan so everything had to be handwashed. I had a big metal bucket that I boiled the nappies up in. So long as we had the gas, of course. But I was so naive about baby things that at first, I even put the soiled nappies in without first sluicing the mess off. I couldn't understand why they didn't come clean! I think that Brenda put me right on that, but not before I'd put Jim's white cricket-style jumper with its green trim in the bucket to boil with the nappies. Well, it was white (apart from the trim). He was not amused.

After a few weeks, Melissa was ill with bronchitis. She went back into hospital and into an oxygen tent. It was a worrying time, but fortunately, after about a week, she was well enough to bring back home. What a relief that was.

Just a few days after that, we got a huge surprise. There was a knock on the caravan door, and when we opened it, there stood Jim's mum and dad and our old mate Chris! Jim's brother must have told them where we were as we'd had no contact since our hasty retreat a few months before.

They seemed so pleased to see us, hugging and kissing us both, and of course, they were overjoyed to meet their new little granddaughter. They were also very concerned to hear she had just come out of hospital after her bout of bronchitis.

"It must be because of the cold damp caravan you're living in," my mother-in-law stated. It was cold and damp and the middle of winter. "You can't stay here. You must come home with us. You can fit them in the car, can't you Chris?"

I really didn't want to leave our first little home and remembered how difficult it had been the previous times living with his parents. But despite anything I said, Jim was all for going back. I found out later that he'd hardly paid any rent since we'd lived there and we were due to be evicted soon anyway. Although I didn't know it at the time, I suppose it was our only option. Brenda had just had her baby, so that was probably enough for her to cope with, without us going back there and Jim being out of work too.

So we packed everything up and put as much as we could in the boot of Chris's car. Of course, we couldn't get our big pram in the car so Jim put it in a shed on the site, along with anything else we couldn't fit in the car. We had a yellow baby bath that I loaded up with all my personal bits—letters, photos, various papers, and my treasured make-up bag—but it just wouldn't fit in the car, and unbeknown to me at the time, this went into the shed too.

Jim said he would get his brother to pick everything up later for us, but we never saw any of it again.

CHAPTER 13

Parents Again

ONCE WE'D SETTLED BACK IN his parents' place, we still found that, as nobody worked, money was very tight. When I would talk to Jim to encourage him to find work or to tell him of a job I'd seen advertised, his mum would jump in and say angrily that it wasn't a woman's place to talk like that to her husband.

Eventually, Jim's mother and I got a job working together delivering leaflets. We would get picked up at ten in the morning, and after our day's work, we were dropped off again about 5 p.m., five days a week. While we were working, Jim and his dad looked after little Melissa. Then his mum took a second job, working evenings as a cook in a local pub. She certainly was an excellent cook and a hard worker.

We asked about the layette set that we'd left behind, but they said they hadn't seen it and we must have left it at the caravan. We found out not long after that they'd actually gifted it to Raif and Brenda when she'd had her second baby. So from one wedding present, we went down to none.

One evening, Jim said to me that because we never had any time to ourselves, it would be a good idea to go out for a nice walk together. There was no dog to walk anymore, sadly. We just walked around the local roads, then he brought me back via the Council garages, which I thought was an odd choice. Then to my surprise, he shoved me roughly against a garage door and started thrusting himself against me. No foreplay, just a very rough grabbing and pulling me about like a rag doll. I was really frightened—and worried in case someone came along to use their garage. He kept at it for what seemed like ages and wouldn't listen when I begged him to stop and to go back home. I was crying by the end of it and glad when we did finally go home.

"Did you have a nice walk?" they asked. Of course, we said yes.

Several nights a week, we went for our "walk". I tried all excuses to get out of going in case the same happened again. Tired. Headache. Something on TV. But Jim invariably got his own way, and even his mum said I should be an obedient wife and go. And the same thing did happen, every time. More than once he drew blood, bashing my head against the wall or on the floor if he pushed me right down. I was so frightened. I didn't understand his behaviour. I just wanted the old Jim back.

After a while, our relationship with his parents started to disintegrate again. Everything I did in the house, from helping with the housework to looking after my baby, his mother criticised. One day, his mother was so incensed about something that she snatched Melissa out of my arms. That was the last straw. I contacted my own parents for the first time in well over a year and told them that we were at Jim's parents' house but we just couldn't stay there anymore. Could we please come and stay with them instead? I knew that wouldn't be easy either as they both hated Jim, but it was a bigger house so we wouldn't be under their feet all the time. They actually agreed and said we could have our own bedroom and living room while we were there.

So we left his parents and went to mine, some ten miles away. I didn't actually relish the thought of going back there, but I knew we would have much more privacy and there would be no rowing or shouting every day.

I was about five months' pregnant again when we moved in with my parents, and it was the first time they had seen my Melissa. They fell in love with her straight away. Through the day, my mother used to say, "Leave your living room door open so Melissa can come in and see me." And she would toddle in and out between our two living rooms, which were next to each other. Sometimes she took Melissa into the garden with her.

I didn't get too much bad treatment from Jim while we were living there, although he was very rough and aggressive in our lovemaking and it definitely wasn't a pleasure. I didn't see much of him though. He had two or three different short-lived jobs while we were there and would often go out for the evening, after his dinner. My parents noticed this and asked about it. I didn't want them to think badly of him, so I would make up excuses as I didn't really know where he went. While there, he joined a men's hockey team, so that accounted for two evenings a week. My parents reckoned that was rubbish as that was a girl's game, they said. He did bring home a hockey stick so it could've been true, though I never saw him play.

One afternoon, Jim came home and said he'd take Melissa and me swimming, and he brandished a pound note in the air, which would cover the cost. He put the pound on the coffee table and I went upstairs to get our swimming things together. When I came back down, he said, "Right. Are we ready?" We were, but when he went to pick up the money, it had gone! He asked if I'd put it in my purse, but I hadn't. We spent a long time looking for it, and Jim was getting madder by the minute, cursing and swearing. I really hoped my mother couldn't hear him from the next room.

In the end, he was so angry he picked up Melissa's plastic toy tortoise and hurled it across the room, whereupon the tortoise's removable hat flew off, and there inside its head was the missing pound note! Little Melissa must have poked it in there when we weren't looking. We did go swimming and laughed about it for a long time afterwards!

Melissa said her first word while we were living there. Loudly and clearly, she said, "Shit." I was rather upset about this as I didn't swear, not even mildly. Jim thought it was hilarious and said she must've got it from me. I just hoped she didn't say it in front of her nan. One morning while I was getting her dressed, I suddenly became aware of what I was saying to her. On went her vest. "That's it," I said. Then her petticoat. "That's it." Then her dress. "That's it" again. Then finally her little knitted cardigan went on, and a last "That's it." That's when I realised my little Melissa wasn't swearing at all. She was just copying me and saying, "That's it"!

When my second baby was due, I went into labour during the night. I couldn't wake Jim up so I sat rocking and moaning on the stairs. My dad heard and came to see what was the matter. I think it was probably obvious! Anyhow, he managed to wake Jim and sent him off to call for an ambulance. No mobile phones back then, and not everyone had house phones either. The nearest public telephone box was about ten minutes away, and he ran there and back as fast as he could. Apparently, when he got there, he realised he hadn't got any money for the call, but the garage opposite was open and they felt sorry for him and let him call from there.

I was just booked into hospital for two days as now there was a choice of how long we could stay, and I felt I didn't need to be shown everything all over again. I must have been very noisy in the labour room because the next morning, the new mums on my ward said they'd heard me yelling!

This time I had a dear, little, blond boy, and we called him Scott. Still no flowers, chocolates, or balloons from Jim, but as ever, he had no job and no money.

Not long after Scott was born, we had a discussion with my parents, who agreed to write a letter to the local Council to say they couldn't have us living there any longer as my dad's health was not good. We hoped that by doing this, the Council would house us.

We weren't housed straight away though. We were put in a little hotel in Eltham, and we had to pay a small amount of rent to the Council, as this was a scheme organised to help homeless people. But at least it was a roof over our heads, and not with family. It wasn't an easy time though as we had to be off the premises between ten in the morning and six in the evening, with our two babies, whatever the weather, and I remember it rained a lot. We had to eat in cafes or buy our own food to make up a picnic. Also, I had to do all our washing in the little sink in our room, even the nappies.

We were only there for about three weeks when we were reassigned to the New Hackwood Hotel in Bromley. A much bigger and grander hotel than the Eltham one. This was much better for us as we didn't have to leave the hotel as we had done before. We just had to vacate our room for an hour through the morning, for the cleaners. There was a big lounge there with a TV, and we could sit in there any time, or stay in our rooms once the cleaners had been.

I had regularly written to Jim's parents after we left there as I felt it was the right thing to do, regardless of the fact that we left on bad terms. When they heard we were in Bromley, they had us over a couple of times a week for dinner and to do our laundry. In a proper twin tub at last and not the hotel bedroom sink! We would walk over to theirs, a good hour's walk, but we were both young and able. They were so happy to see little Melissa again and to meet her little brother Scott. Jim's mother had a kind heart. Sometimes I loved her, and other times I couldn't stand her! But two visits a week was fine, and no drama ensued.

One day while we were visiting them for our dinner, there was a knock on the door and Jim's dad went to answer it. We couldn't hear everything that was said, but we did hear a man's stern voice asking for James Jones. Then we heard his dad shouting, "It's my son, and I've no idea where he is! He's buggered off, and you can bugger off too!" Apparently, the man ripped his papers up there and then and closed the case. It was a debt collector for Burtons, his dad told us when he came back in. They all laughed, but I felt really bad when I remembered the lovely suit that Jim had worn on our wedding day. It all seemed so dishonest. I didn't dare say anything though.

While staying at the New Hackwood Hotel, Jim managed to get a job as a barman there. This meant I didn't see much of him through the evenings. It was quite lonely up in our room once the babies were asleep. I couldn't leave them; otherwise, I could have gone back down to the lounge to watch television. I was quite bored.

While working there, Jim made friends with the manager and some of the regulars who came in. He even started to go out through the daytime with his new friends, and I missed him even more then. There was a big party of young people down from Scotland staying there one week, and straight away, Jim made friends with them and started going out with them every day and when he had an evening off. He even went to London ice skating with them one day. This really upset me because ice skating had been my favourite thing of all. I didn't know he was going until he came back and told me they'd been. They went to all sorts of places, including Madame Tussauds and the

Tower of London. I knew there were several girls in this party and wondered how well Jim had got to know them—and more importantly if he'd behaved. I have to say I was very relieved when they all went back to Scotland.

CHAPTER 14

Housed at Last

AFTER A FEW MONTHS OF hotel accommodation, we were at last housed in a little end of terrace cottage in Sidcup. We were thrilled. Our first proper home. We were told it was just temporary as the row of old houses was due for demolition later that year, so when that happened, they would rehouse us again.

The first thing I did when we were there, and in a more settled situation, was to contact the local Bible group. I knew where it was because I'd visited their group a few years previously. They were so welcoming. It was as if I'd never lost contact. A few there I already knew, and I made lots of new friends too.

Jim wouldn't come to their meetings with me though, and that made me sad. I still hadn't got the "real" Jim back. I started to wonder if this coarse, dirty-minded, dishonest, and work-shy man was the real Jim and the one I'd first met was the Jim who was putting on an act. The realisation of this broke my heart. I didn't love him, but I knew I was bound to him through marriage, which I believed was a sacred arrangement. And despite everything, I still felt for him and wanted to make him happy. And of course, he was the father of my babies.

When we first moved there, Jim still had his job at the hotel, but at least now I was at home in my own little place. We had rented a TV, we had a radio, and I joined the library. Also, I had the Bible group's meetings, so there was plenty to do when he was working.

One evening after work, Jim came back with someone in a car. They came in and promptly unplugged our rented television, loaded it onto the back seat of the car, and then drove off. A couple of hours later, Jim came back again, and I asked him what he was playing at. He said the hotel manager was upset because the recreation room television was broken, so he'd said he'd get him one cheap.

"Our one?" I queried. "But it's only rented."

"Don't worry. I've got a plan," he replied.

A few nights later, Jim went out for a couple of hours and brought the television back. I was so relieved.

The following night he went back to work, and he told me later, laughing as he did, that the manager had said, "Jim, you know that lovely television you sold me? Well, some blighter's stolen it!" He probably said something a lot worse than blighter too.

I loved our first little house. It was tiny, with just two bedrooms. The front door opened straight onto the living room, and through there was a little kitchen with a bathroom and toilet off that. No front garden, but a little one out the back with a beautiful, yellow laburnum tree in it. In the corner of the living room was a cute, little, built-in cupboard painted white, which housed the gas meter. It had a shelf on the top that I dusted every day and displayed my few little knick-knacks on there.

One day the gas man called to empty the cash from the meter for the first time. At last, someone to show off my much-loved cupboard and shelf to. I let him in and opened the cupboard door with a flourish. He got on his knees to do his job, then promptly stood back up and declared, "This gas meter's empty!" Boy, was I embarrassed! I had no idea, and I began to realise even more just how dishonest my husband was.

One day while living there, I started to feel really unwell. I lay down on the floor and must've passed out. Jim came home and found me there, with baby Scott *gooing* in his pram and little Melissa, barely two, piling cups, saucers, plates, and the like all up into a big tower. Amazingly, nothing was broken! I was whisked off in an ambulance to hospital, where I was diagnosed with viral meningitis. I don't remember how long I was in hospital for, but once back home, I soon recovered, with no lasting effects thankfully.

We didn't live in that house for very long. In fact, we moved into two different houses in Sidcup after that. The next house was also for a very brief time as that row of houses was being demolished as well.

Our last Sidcup move, still temporary accommodation, was a house just round the corner, so with us, our neighbours, and Jim's mates he'd made at the local pub, we carried everything round to the new house on foot. We must have looked a funny crew. (Steptoe comes to mind again.)

Once we'd settled into our new house, I discovered that I was pregnant again. It wasn't planned, and the contraception we used hadn't worked. Much as I loved children, I was worried because we never had any money, although Jim did have his own ideas of getting some extra cash.

I realised exactly what he was doing when Jim loaded our rented television onto Scott's pram. He put a blanket over it then wheeled it off somewhere and sold it. When he came back, he reported it as stolen to the rental company, and as the company was insured, they rented us another one. He must have done this at least half a dozen times and hired from all the rental shops in the area. I felt we were lucky to still be able to rent one. Surely, they would catch up with him eventually.

The pram came in useful to Jim for something else too. Jim started having parties every weekend, after the local pub closed. He would come home at the end of the evening with twenty or so pub mates and demand that I get back up from my bed and play hostess, making sandwiches for them. I didn't even know them.

Sometimes I pretended I was asleep to get out of it, but that rarely worked. Then the following morning, he would gather up all the empty beer bottles, load them on the pram, and wheel them off to get the money back on the empties, which used to be a little pocket moneymaker back then.

I hated that he was at the pub so much when we had so little money. He'd often come home late and drunk and throw his dinner up the wall. Then he'd come up to the bedroom and demand that I get up and make him something else to eat. What I'd left for him for dinner was disgusting, he would say. More than once he came back from the pub, came up to the bedroom, and threw a beer glass at me. One time he split my head open and I had to go to hospital to have it stitched up. Jim knocked up one of our neighbours to babysit, telling him I'd had a nasty accident, then he walked me up to the hospital that fortunately was very close by. He told the hospital staff that I'd had some sort of accident and played the caring husband while we were there. After I was stitched up, he walked me down the hill back home.

But that too was an ordeal. He kept pushing me into the bushes and pulling me about. I just wanted to get home and back in my bed. My head hurt badly, and I was terribly upset. But that wasn't all. Jim had a strange obsession with me going to the toilet. He wanted me to walk down the hill in front of him and wet myself. I couldn't think of anything worse, even though there wasn't anyone else about that late at night. I couldn't do it to order. But he just wouldn't let me go home. He kept messing me about by the hedge for a long time and pushing me into it. He kept begging me and saying that if I loved him, I would do it to please him. In the end, I thought the only way to get back home was to do it and get it over and done with. So I did. It felt awful.

When we finally got home, Jim sent the babysitter away, then took me to the bathroom where he stripped me off and spent a long time washing me down. I hated every minute of it and felt very humiliated.

His treatment of me worsened. I became very frightened of him and had many more trips to the hospital for stitches, as well as for some minor fractures, which he'd caused by his brutal treatment.

I remember more than once the police coming, because my screams had been reported while we were out of an evening, but seeing that we were husband and wife, it was never taken any further. That's how it was in the seventies.

At one point, I couldn't stand it anymore so I packed a bag, put the two children in the pram, and walked to the local police station. I told them we were homeless because of the volatile situation at home. They consequently sent us to a "safe house" in the next town, where we were allocated a room for ourselves and joint use of the kitchen and bathroom. By this time, I was bordering on a breakdown.

But Jim found us after two days. I don't know how, but by some crafty means no doubt, and he came and took us back home. I didn't have the strength to fight and went back like a lamb.

Shortly after I'd returned home, I gave birth to my third baby. Another little blond boy we called Mark. Again, no flowers or goodies from Jim, but my friends from the Bible group sent me cards and some hand-knitted jumpers. They had no idea of my situation or circumstances with my husband. It would be too embarrassing to tell them.

It was around this time that I started seeing the doctor because of my breakdown and was prescribed antidepressants. This led to several overdoses, some intentional, as I just couldn't bear my life anymore, though some accidental as I gradually became zombielike. This was when Jim got a workmate's girlfriend, Janice, in to look after me as mentioned in the opening chapter. But this wasn't very successful, and by this time, our neighbours and associates thought (with some help from Jim) that I was mentally unstable. I suppose by now I was.

On one occasion, probably before Janice came to stay, there were almost dire consequences from my overdose attempt. Apparently, when my husband returned home from work, I was lying unconscious on the dining room floor. He switched on the television, made himself a cup of tea, and sat completely ignoring me. After a while, our next-door neighbour, Moira, popped in for a chat, as she sometimes did, and Jim offered her a cup of tea.

"But what's Helen doing on the floor like that?" Moira asked.

"Silly cow's taken another overdose. Leave her."

"You can't just leave her there, Jim?"

"If she wants to kill herself, let her get on with it. Have a cup of tea, Moira."

But Moira wouldn't just leave me. She tried to bring me round, but without success. Now Moira was a big strong woman, built like a female wrestler, and she picked me up bodily, leaving my husband drinking his tea.

She carried me out through the front door, where she stood me up, put an arm around my waist, and walked me, still in my unconscious state, up the road for some fresh air. We lived on a main road, a bus route, though fortunately it was a Sunday so presumably not too busy.

After a while, a police car came by and stopped, wanting to know what was going on. We must've looked pretty odd, and I don't know whether someone observing us had alerted the police or if they had driven by us purely by chance. Either way, they picked us up and drove us to the local hospital, where I was given a stomach pump then placed in the intensive care unit, still unconscious.

I have no idea how long I was in the intensive care bed, but as I started to regain consciousness, my heart literally skipped a beat and I immediately thought, *I'm dead!* Then I realised that if I were dead, I wouldn't be able to think it. So slowly, and disappointed, I opened my eyes to discover that my chest was covered in wires. Beside me was a television monitor showing a zigzagging line. I could not avert my eyes from that monitor. I knew that if the zigzag line stopped, then I would be dead. But it wouldn't, and it didn't stop.

I must have drifted in and out of consciousness some more, and when I came properly round, my husband was there. I was going to have the wires removed and be sent to one of the general wards, but my husband insisted on taking me home with him straight away. He said he could give me twenty-four hours a day care and attention and would not leave my side until I was back on my feet. After signing me out of the hospital and intensive care unit, completely against the advice of the medical staff, he put his arm around me in much the same way as my neighbour must have done earlier, and in that way, I was taken back into the nightmare.

The next step was for me to see a psychiatrist. No one else could fathom out why I was so depressed and unstable. So now, as well as regular trips with split head, broken bones, and overdoses, I was at the hospital every week, seeing a nice, friendly, African psychiatrist. At least I think he was nice and friendly. I couldn't understand much of what he said. His rich African accent sounded like a foreign language to me! I did get that he was asking about my home life, but I didn't say much except to tell him about my kind, caring husband who always walked me up the lane for my hospital appointments and waited patiently to take me home again. In fact, he never let me take the fifteen-minute walk there or back alone. He was ever the "dutiful" husband whom I loved dearly, didn't I?

During these early years with Jim, he seemed always to be claiming to be ill. And if someone else said they had a headache, stomach ache, or sore throat, he would say, "Yes, so have I." And his was supposedly much worse. Several times I'd had to call the doctor out for him. Once when he collapsed on the stairs and I couldn't rouse him, I called an ambulance. He was taken to hospital, given an enema, then sent back home with a clean bill of health.

Another time he went into hospital, howling in agony. They could find nothing wrong, and after a day or two of tests, they said he could go home. I brought his clothes back up later that day and pulled the screens around the bed so he could get dressed. But before he'd finished dressing, he collapsed back on the bed, screaming. The nurses came running, helped him back into bed, and called the doctor to come quickly. He had to have an emergency exploratory operation, but they still found nothing wrong. In fact, this happened several times over the years, and I realised it must be all in his mind.

One time was genuine though. He had an abscess in one of his testicles and went into hospital. They drained the abscess, and after a day or two, they discharged him and organised for a district nurse to come to our home to clean and dress the wound. When she came, she gave me a prescription to take to the chemist for some antibiotics and a surgical strap for him.

I asked, "What's a surgical strap?"

She said, "Don't worry about it. The chemist will know."

So I dutifully went to the local chemist and handed over the prescription. The assistant called out loudly from the back room, "What size jockstrap do you want?" I nearly died on the spot with embarrassment in front of the other customers. His were the only testicles I'd ever seen, so I actually had no idea what size he needed.

In the end, Jim had to go back into hospital to have the testicle completely removed, and he had a prosthesis one put in. But for some reason, that was unsatisfactory. He had to go back in and have the prosthesis removed. So in all, he went into hospital three or four times until he was completely discharged. He took a lot of stick from his mates at the pub because of it. But I think he enjoyed it. He loved being the centre of attention, and this was a great excuse for lots of crude jokes for weeks afterwards.

Jim continued to treat me badly, and my own trips to the accident and emergency department continued. Although I was too frightened to tell them the truth behind my "accidents", I did wonder, *Surely they have their suspicions about them?* But nothing was ever said, and no questions were asked, so I just continued on, taking my antidepressants.

I was still occasionally taking overdoses because I felt so depressed and desperate. There were plenty of tablets to be taken. Either my own or Jim's as he always had a stock of various medications and painkillers in the house. But when I did, it made Jim even angrier with me, so life was just unbearable. He seemed to be so angry all the time that it was like treading on eggshells. But my children kept me going. They were all under 3 years old and were so close and loving towards each other. My eldest, Melissa, was so caring and helpful to her little brothers, even at that young age, and I loved them all so much it must have been what kept me going.

Jim said that he loved me. No one else had ever said that, so I had to be grateful. That dutiful husband who always looked after me. Wasn't it every little girl's dream to grow up and be loved, get married, and have a family? I'd done that. I'd got married. I'd been loved. I'd got my family. So why didn't I feel like a "real person"?

CHAPTER 15

On the Buses

THEN SURPRISE SURPRISE—JIM GOT A job! He became a bus conductor, and he seemed to enjoy it. He made lots of friends with the other conductors and drivers and would often play pool with them at the garage after work. He also brought them home sometimes during his break as we lived very near the bus garage in Footscray. There were some social events too that we all went to, such as football and cricket matches. We also got invited to various house parties. I always liked the idea of a party, especially as I loved music and dancing. Our neighbour was always available to babysit, but I wasn't treated very well. Jim would never dance with me, though he would dance with every other girl there, and I found that hurtful.

I soon started to dread these parties. The end of the evening was the worst. On the way home, he would start pulling me about and grabbing my legs to make me fall, so he could jump on top of me for some rough sex, out in the open, regardless of where we were.

One of the first friends Jim made on the buses was a driver called Terry, who was just filling in, in between jobs. I don't remember what his actual job was, but he was also the drummer at weekends in a local band called the Ramburgers. Jim started to go with them to help them set up their equipment at the various working men's clubs where they played. I thought this sounded wonderful as I love music of all kinds and had never seen a live band play. So I begged Jim to let me go with him.

We organised for our babysitter to come, and it really was so much fun. I met the rest of the band, and the singer's girlfriend, Sally, and

I am a Real Person

she and I had the job of starting the dancing off while the Ramburgers played the pop songs of the time as well as some golden oldies. The lead guitarist, who we called H, was a brilliant musician. Whenever he played his solo of Jimi Hendrix's "Red House", almost the entire club would stop what they were doing to listen, and he would get huge applause when he'd finished. Not least of all from me.

But it wasn't just his playing that got to me. I thought he was absolutely gorgeous! He was tall, slim, fair-haired, and handsome. He was the quiet one of the group so I never actually spoke to him after the initial introduction, me being quite shy as well. I had no intention of getting to know him really. I just looked forward to the weekend gigs so I could admire him from a distance.

That little dream bubble burst one evening though when he brought his wife and two small boys to a gig with him. His wife was small, dark, and very, very pretty. When I realised who she was, I went off into the ladies and had a little cry. Nobody knew, and there was no really sensible reason for this.

Another time, the Ramburgers were playing at our local working men's club just ten minutes from where we lived. We went along to help, without needing a lift to get there. As the evening wore on, I started to get a really bad headache and asked Jim to take me home. But he wouldn't leave the club, so I just took myself as it wasn't far.

I'd only been home a short while, sent the babysitter home, and was just going upstairs to bed when there was a knock on the door. It was Mick, the singer from the band. He said he'd just come to check that I was all right. I was most surprised. I assured him I was, and he leaned forward to give me what I thought would be a peck on the cheek goodbye. But suddenly it became a full-blown, passionate, open-mouth kiss! Then he turned without saying another word and went back to the club.

It had felt so good, with no underlying threat attached, but then I realised just how vulnerable I was. I didn't want to do anything wrong because I was married to Jim and that was my lot. And if he found out, he'd be furious. However, it was never mentioned again when we saw Mick and the band. I wondered if Mick had been drunk and had forgotten all about it, if he'd felt embarrassed, or if he wished it had never happened. Of course, it shouldn't have happened, and although it gave me a lovely, warm memory to keep, it never happened again.

On the way home from these gigs, I had to endure all the pulling about and knocking over and rough treatment before we got home. So much as I enjoyed these gigs with the dancing, singing along, and spending time with our Ramburgers friends, I always dreaded going home at the end of the evening. It was rarely any different.

Jim surprised me on our wedding anniversary one year. He'd got tickets for a London West End show. We left our children with the babysitter and went up on the train. First, we had an Indian meal in a restaurant, which was really lovely, then went on to the theatre to watch *Billy Liar* with Michael Crawford in the lead role. It was a brilliant play and very funny.

When we left the theatre, Jim walked me down by the river, stopped by the wall of the embankment, and started kissing me. I dreaded what would follow. I just wanted to get our train back home. Although it was June, it was very cold by the river. I only had a light jacket on and begged him to take me to the train station as I was cold and tired. I don't know how long we were there by the river. A lot of people were going by; after all, it was London. Then he picked me up and sat me on the wall of the embankment. I was not comfortable with this. Then he started pushing me as if he was going to push me over the wall and into the river. I was terrified. Then he'd pull me back, pull my dress up, and maul me about before seeming to push me over again. I thought if that happened, I would die as I was too cold and tired to struggle or fight. It was like a living nightmare and felt like it went on for eternity.

Eventually, he did take me to the station, but even on the train home, he kept pulling me about. All I wanted to do was go to sleep until we got to our station, but that was never happening.

Our evenings out—the theatre trip, evenings in the local pub, or out with our friends in the band—always ended the same and always spoilt the evening for me. As mentioned earlier, they did sometimes result in hospital trips for me.

Jim continued to bring his workmates from the buses home during his breaktimes. But now, once they'd got their cups of tea from me, they would disappear upstairs to the back bedroom. I could hear a strange buzzing noise coming from the room, and when they came out fifteen or so minutes later, they would all be grinning. In time I discovered what they were up to in that bedroom. Jim had designed a method by which to scam some money from the bus company. Somehow, they were winding their conductor's machines backwards, and they'd make maybe a tenner or so each for themselves. That was a lot of money back then.

But Jim's luck ran out. The law caught up with him. A couple of the other bus conductors got caught too, but as the ringleader, Jim was in the most trouble. He told me later that when they first took him to the police station, they asked, "You know what we want you for, don't you?" "No," he said, playing dumb. So they took him into another room, and there, in the middle of the table, was a conductor's ticket machine.

"Right. Show us how it's done," they said.

But he refused to.

He did time inside for it. I forget how long for now, but quite a few months. Apparently, the television business had caught up with him as well, and I believe it was all dealt with together.

I actually enjoyed him being away. It meant that I had some peace and was gradually able to catch up with our rent. Jim was irresponsible with money and we had been threatened with eviction more than once.

A sense of duty made me visit him in Wandsworth prison once a month; in fact, my father took me up on the train the first time to show me where to go. I also wrote to him there and enclosed little notes and pictures from the children, who were now at school.

The children's school was a three-quarters of an hour's walk away, mostly along main roads, one of which we lived in. But it was a good school, and the nearest, and the children were happy there. Sometimes I took my neighbour's boy Danny when his dad didn't drive him there. He was a nice, little boy, close in age to mine, but he was always very grubby. At school, as soon as he arrived, the school nurse would give him a bath and put him into clean clothes and wash his grubby ones. I suppose Danny accepted this as normal. And his mum never queried it either.

One day we were walking to school, and he stopped and had a real good scratch of his bottom.

"Don't do that," I said.

"My auntie Rita says I've got worms," he replied.

"Well, I expect you have" was all I could think to say, and I made a mental note to check my own three after school.

While Jim was in Wandsworth, I became quite ill with dreadful pack pains and headaches. I was diagnosed as having fibrositis, possibly brought on by emotional stress and depression. Although my life was considerably easier now with Jim away, I suppose the stresses of my life up until then must have just caught up with me. I was put on medication and complete bed rest. Fortunately, I could stay home to rest and be with the children.

During this illness, my Melissa was such a little treasure. She was only 7 years old, and in the mornings, she would help her little brothers to dress and make them breakfast of cereal and milk, then she would walk them to school along the busy roads. There was a lollipop lady on the way, and Melissa knew to always cross with her.

After about a week, my neighbours farther down the road noticed Melissa taking her little brothers to school and decided to take advantage of it. When they saw her coming, they would poke their children out of the door to go along with her. It was a while before I found out what they were doing, and I was very upset that they should push so much responsibility on my little girl. I don't think Melissa actually minded though, as she always loved taking charge of little ones, and they always seemed to listen to her. Anyhow, they must have all arrived at school safely and on time as I never heard otherwise.

Melissa didn't relinquish her responsibilities when she got home from school. Her next job was to make some sandwiches for their tea. Thank goodness for free school dinners!

On Saturdays while I was ill, she would take a shopping bag, shopping list, and purse and ride the bus up to town and get some shopping from the co-op. For all she was only seven, I don't know how I'd have managed without her.

During this time, I had a visit from Jane Templer, our housing officer. She was sorry to see how poorly I was and made various suggestions of some help I could apply for while I was so ill and with Jim away in prison. She was also very impressed to see that we'd almost made up all of our back rent that had been owing. She did realise that it was not "us" but "me" who had managed that over the months Jim was away. She said that if we could keep it up, we would soon be allocated a proper Council house. That was our dream, to have a proper permanent home for our little family.

I didn't need to apply for the help that Jane Templer had suggested, because soon after that, I was much better and got back into the everyday swing of things.

When Jim first went to prison, I contacted his mates in the band and told them so they would know that he wouldn't be around to help them set up their equipment for a while. I didn't go to any of their gigs either during this time, much as I loved the music. I didn't feel it would be right without Jim. In fact, I didn't go out anywhere, apart from the usual everyday things and the Bible group meetings. I didn't tell my friends there about our situation though. It would be too embarrassing.

But having said that, I did actually go out one night. Mark, the bass player from the Ramburgers, came one evening to cheer me up and took me out for dinner. It was quite unexpected, with no strings attached and no hidden agenda. Mark was a nice, gentle kind of guy, and Jim and I had been to his flat several times to wind down after a gig, so I felt quite comfortable with him.

When he brought me home after our meal, he gave me a little peck on the cheek, like he always did, and I thanked him and hugged him goodbye. I think I hugged him for a lot longer than I should have, though there was nothing more than that, and he left. I remember realising then just how starved of affection I was and had been, even when Jim was home.

When he was due home from prison, I made some decorations with the children and put them up, along with balloons and homemade posters saying, "Welcome home, Daddy." They were so excited. I had mixed feelings. Part of me dreaded it, but a little part of me hoped that his time inside would have changed him for the better somehow.

He was, of course, really glad to be home and made a huge fuss of us all. He asked how I'd managed, so I said fine and told him that one of our friends, Mark, from the band, had come to see how I was, and took me out to dinner. How kind was that! But no. Jim was furious. He accused us of having an affair. He even claimed to have seen us kissing in the kitchen of his flat the last time we'd been there. This was of course rubbish. Mark and I didn't have that sort of chemistry, and even if we did, there was no way we'd have been kissing in his kitchen with the door open and my husband in the next room!

We never went to see the Ramburgers play after that. Jim just wouldn't go. However, he did keep in contact with Mick, the singer, and some months later, Mick told us that Mark had disappeared. He'd left his flat and moved back in with his parents, but one day he'd just gone out and no one had seen or heard from him since. He'd even left his most precious possession behind, his guitar. It was certainly odd and made me feel sad. But there was nothing I could do about it, and Jim didn't seem bothered. So that was the end of that. And that was the end of the Ramburgers too, I guess.

Meanwhile, Jim had made quite a name for himself at the bus garage. Because of his scam, all the ticket machines had to be called in and changed, or possibly renewed, bearing in mind that Jim had refused to tell how it was done. It must have cost the bus company a fortune!

CHAPTER 16

Cleaner of the Year

NOW THAT JIM WAS HOME from prison, we were back to square one with precious little income and Jim with no job. He didn't seem in a hurry to find one either, so I found myself a little job working for a company called Showerline. I was one of a team of four girls, and we went from door to door trying to book appointments for our rep to call to try to sell them a shower. I enjoyed working with the girls, but one week, for some reason, none of the other girls could work so my boss, Monty, said he'd pick me up in the morning and we'd go together. I got up and ready, but when he arrived to pick me up, Jim saw him out there in his little sports car and rushed out to speak to him before I'd even got my coat on. Monty then drove off. I've no idea what Jim had said to him, but that was the end of that job.

I managed to get another job. I signed up with an agency that sent me to work in a typing pool. It was quite a boring job, as I didn't have a clue as to what I was typing. I just had to set it out as I was shown and copy it accurately. I think I did OK. I was paid monthly, but Jim cleverly managed to get my first month's wages off me and spent it all on a large tent so we could go on holiday with the children. Unfortunately, it meant we were still very skint for the next month, so my next month's wages had to pay off all the previous month's debts. I didn't see any of that money either.

I lost heart with that job and tried a couple of others. One was in a stockroom helping out, then one was in an office, both jobs with weekly pay, which I hoped would be better. Unfortunately, they were only temporary jobs and didn't last long.

Around this time, our neighbour Roy, Danny's dad and Moira's husband, started to take a keen interest in photography. Every time we left our house, there he was with his camera, taking photos of his car, his front garden, the factory next door to him, or the shop by us.

One day Roy decided he'd like to have a go at photographing people and asked me to be his model. I asked what it would involve, as he was a bit of a shady character, and although I was flattered to be asked, I certainly didn't want any scantily clad pictures of me—or worse! He assured me that he just wanted some full face and side face pictures, and I was ideal "because you're pretty". Wow! Someone thought I was pretty! I was sold.

I was then quite happy to put on my make-up and do my hair nicely and be photographed. He also took a lot of full-body shots too, so my prettiest dresses came out for that. Moira didn't seem to mind. She said she didn't want to be in any pictures. Possibly because she was an extremely large lady, but also she never seemed to have time for her husband's hobbies and interests anyway.

I have to say the photographs were really good, although of course, it was just amateur stuff. But I was still proud to say I was a model! When my Melissa was in her early teens, she had grown into a bit of a beanpole and got teased at school for it. So I told her to tell the children, "My mum's tall and skinny too, and she was a model!" I hope it helped.

Jim and I then got a job together. It was from Monday to Friday, ten until four, cleaning in a large office complex. It gave us time to get the children to school first, and we gave Melissa a door key as they would get home a good half hour before us. Their instructions were to come in, get a drink of squash and a packet of crisps, then sit down and watch television until we got back.

There were a lot of offices where we were working, but our job was just to clean the toilets and restrooms, although I did have to walk through some of the offices with my mop and bucket. I used to feel embarrassed, because I knew I could do office work just as well as anyone else. I didn't enjoy being a cleaner, but we needed the money and the job was there.

I am a Real Person

One afternoon, we came home from work to find Roy in our front garden, photographing our cat Boots. He grinned up at us, knowing we wouldn't mind.

Then Jim had what he thought was a great idea. "How about you lend me your camera tonight so I can take some family photos, Roy?"

While they were discussing this, our front door opened, and Melissa came running out, followed by her brothers. "Dad! Dad!"

"Go back in and watch tele."

"But Dad—"

"We'll be in in a minute. Go and watch tele."

"Dad, but where *is* the tele?" Melissa stuttered.

We rushed in, followed by Roy and Boots, and there, where the television should have been, was an empty TV stand. Roy swore he hadn't seen anyone at our house, and we were quite baffled, although I think we both were a little bit suspicious of him. But we still went round asking our neighbours if they'd seen anything. Nobody had, until we asked in the general store next to us. The shopkeeper said she'd seen a man in a white overall coming round the side of our house carrying a television, which he put in a white van and drove off. At the time, she thought nothing of it, assuming it was a television repairman we had called in.

The white overall and van did give us a big clue as to who it was. Some dodgy, so-called pal of Jim's from the pub, who would have known we'd all be out at that time of day. However, it was nothing we could prove. So if it was him, he got away with it with his boldness. I didn't dare say it at the time, but I did think that Jim had got a taste of his own medicine!

Although Roy had brought a couple of his cameras round a bit later, Jim was so angry about the television business that he was in no mood to photograph the children. I thought it was a shame, although I understood. He kept on at me to put them to bed. They went early anyway, as they were only little, but I took them up a bit earlier than usual and sat with them singing and reading for a while. I knew they too were rather unsettled about the missing television and their dad's angry outbursts about it.

I could hear one of Jim's Pink Floyd albums playing downstairs, so I expected to spend the rest of the evening listening to music with him as he had a big collection of LPs. But that wasn't the case.

"What's all this for?" I asked when I came back downstairs and went into the living room.

He'd got some curtains draped over the settee and on the floor, and I could see a small pile of my fanciest underwear on the arm of the settee. It didn't take me long to realise just what he had planned, the biggest clue being him fiddling with one of Roy's cameras as I came into the room.

I really didn't want to cooperate. It seemed wrong because he hadn't felt like photographing the children earlier, so why me now? What was so different? The obvious, I supposed. I just didn't want to, but I knew there would be no point in arguing with him, although I did try.

I wasn't comfortable with the saucy shots that he wanted, despite the fact that he was my husband and that no one else was in the room. The other thing that worried me was the developing of these photos later on. I asked Jim about that, and he said Roy would show him how to do it in his darkroom next door, then he'd leave him to get on with it. I wasn't sure I believed that. But he bullied me into posing for him. At least I had my undies on, even if they were a bit skimpy.

At first, I was just sitting sweetly in my underwear, smiling at the camera, but after a while, he wanted me to touch myself intimately. I didn't want to do that. After a lot of pleading and sobbing from me, and several slaps from Jim, he got his own way. Next, he ripped my underwear off and gave me our long-handled bath brush, which he just happened to have handy, and insisted I play with that, rubbing it and poking it in myself. It made me cry, and I still to this day can't say any more about that humiliation except that it made me feel sick and some of this is now blocked from my memory. By now it was gone midnight and I just wanted to go to bed.

But that wasn't going to happen yet. Jim then produced some towels that he also had handy, and now he wanted me to wet myself. He put one of the towels underneath me. I was getting used to having to do this for him, even though I hated it and hated myself for doing it. But the truth was I was frightened of him and what he would do to me if I didn't comply. I'd had his huge hands around my throat many times for refusing, and it took all my strength to fight him off. This night was no different. Everything afterwards on that night is a blur in my memory now, and I've no idea what time we finally went to bed.

After work the next day, Jim returned the camera to Roy and took the films round for developing. He later swore blind that Roy had just shown him how to do it, then had left him to get on with it. I wasn't sure that I believed him and was frightened to look our neighbour in the eye for a long time after, in case he had seen.

Jim showed me the photos of me in my underwear. For what they were, they were actually quite tasteful, although I certainly didn't want anyone else seeing them. The rest of the photos Jim said were for his eyes only, and he wouldn't even let me see them. I didn't want to see them anyway and wished he would destroy them. Or better still, wished I'd never done it in the first place. I couldn't get my head around why I had let him do it. I felt he was in complete control of my life. I had no choice in anything. A nothing person.

The next day, we went to work as usual. There were six of us cleaners working there: one other woman and three other men, all a lot older than us. We were still in our 20s while they were pensioners working to supplement their pension. They were a jolly lot, and the men in particular always had a funny story or a joke to tell. On the site, there was a cleaner's hut, which was actually a caravan where we went for our tea breaks and at lunchtimes.

This particular day, I headed to the caravan at twelve for my lunch, and as I walked in, they all looked at me and giggled. I frowned at Jim, who just looked the other way, then I saw that the others were all looking from me, to the wall, and back again. And what was on the wall that they were looking at? Me! A blown-up photo of me! In my skimpy underwear, with a big sign next to it that stated, "Cleaner of the Year 1978!"

CHAPTER 17

Camping

TO MAKE AMENDS, JIM SAID he'd take me and the children away in the tent at the weekend. He said the poster had just been a joke, but to me, it felt more like a betrayal.

He arranged for Roy to drive us to Folkestone on Saturday morning, bringing our tent in his trailer. It wasn't the nicest of journeys because Roy's car smelt badly of petrol, stale food, and body odour, as did he. But it was also quite exciting as it was our first time using the tent and our first time away with the children. Moira said she would feed our cat Boots.

We found a good campsite, and Jim and Roy set up the tent while I watched the children and sorted out all our bits and pieces to go inside. We'd also borrowed a little camping stove to use there.

Once the tent was set up, Roy set off again in his car, and Jim went with him. "To go for a quick beer to thank him," he said.

A long time went by, so I made some lunch of sandwiches for the children. In fact, by the time Jim returned, it was starting to get dark. He was drunk and arrived back armed with several more cans of beer. He also had a big bag of fish and chips that we shared out and had a good and welcome feast before I settled the children in their sleeping bags for the night. I'd been playing and running around with the children all afternoon and felt ready to lie down for the night too.

Jim had other ideas. He decided he wanted the two of us to go for a walk. "Don't be silly," I said. "We can't leave the children!"

He kept on and on at me, and in the end, I agreed to just five minutes round the campsite so we'd hear the children if they woke. There was no way I'd go any farther away than that.

It would probably have taken less than five minutes to walk round the perimeter of the site, but Jim kept stopping every few steps to kiss and cuddle me. He ended up pulling my legs from under me, making me fall heavily on my back, completely winding me. Next, he proceeded to try to initiate drunken sex with me there, outside all the other tents. I was so worried that we'd be seen, and I hated every second of it. At last, he gave up and told me to go back to our tent. He said that he'd be back soon after.

I felt so relieved to be going back to the children, but while hurrying back, suddenly my legs were pulled from under me again, this time with me falling face down. Next, he got on top of me and pushed something over my nose and mouth while forcing himself roughly into my back passage. It was incredibly painful, and I had to use all my strength to push away whatever it was over my face. It was his T-shirt that he'd taken off.

We were struggling there for a long time until he finally gave up, while I was holding back an ocean of tears. Eventually, we went back into the tent, where fortunately the children were still fast asleep. Jim drank the rest of his beers before finally giving in to sleep. Only then did I feel safe enough to relax and go to sleep myself, despite being in a lot of pain. I hoped desperately that nobody had seen us that night.

The next morning Jim acted as if nothing had happened and cooked us a huge breakfast on the little camping stove. We had sausages, eggs, bacon, baked beans, and fried bread, and we all tucked in before going down to the beach for a paddle. The children loved it. It was a rare treat for them. I reminded Jim that he'd promised to buy them a bucket and spade each, but he got very angry with me for mentioning it. He had no money now, he said. I felt so sad for the children. I would never dream of making a promise to them and then breaking it.

We had a little picnic there on the beach at lunchtime. Fishpaste sandwiches and a packet of custard creams to share. Jim disappeared for an hour or so and came back with some cans of beer again. He drank one then fell asleep for the rest of the afternoon. (I thought he had no money.)

While he slept, the children and I played on the sand and in the water. I even managed a little swim while keeping an eye on them.

As the afternoon wore on and the sun disappeared behind the clouds, I felt it was time to pack up and head back to the tent. The only problem was that we couldn't wake their dad up. We shouted at him, the children jumped on him, but he just snorted and rolled over on his towel. I was tempted to leave him there. He'd soon come back when he woke up and found we had gone! But at that suggestion, the children started to cry. He might not have been the best of dads, with all his shouting, getting drunk and breaking promises, but he was *their* dad.

After more jumping on him by the children, pulling at his legs and trying to pull the towel from under him, he eventually woke up, waving his arms and shouting, "What have you done with my beer?" along with some more expletives.

Back at the tent, I suggested it must be about dinnertime. Only then came the realisation that we had eaten the whole day's rations at breakfast, with our huge, full English. There was nothing left for our evening meal. The children started to cry, but Jim said, "Don't worry. I've got a plan." He told the children to stay in the tent and look at their comics they'd brought with them, and then he pushed me out of the tent.

Across from us was a little two-man tent with a young couple in it. We'd waved and said hello to them a couple of times since being there. Jim's plan was for me to go over to them acting all upset and telling them we had no money as I'd lost my purse on the beach. Hopefully, then they would lend us some cash. I protested at this dishonesty. I wasn't going to lie.

"Would you rather the children starved then?" he growled, giving me a shove. He kept on and on until I just stood there crying while he kept pushing me towards their tent.

The young couple must have heard us and came out to see what was wrong.

"Tell them, Helen," Jim demanded.

"We've got no money," I stuttered through my tears.

"And why's that?" Jim snarled.

I couldn't bear the way he was telling me off in front of them, especially when I'd done nothing wrong. So Jim then told them the made-up tale of me losing my purse and now we were stuck with nothing.

His plan worked. They lent us some money and Jim took their address so we could send it back when we got home. I doubted that he would ever return it, and I knew I would never be able to.

After getting the money, Jim set off to find a shop, and I went back in the tent to the children who, fortunately, were totally oblivious to the little scene played out a few yards away.

Jim returned in a short while with some more beers, some cigarettes, and a big bag of chips to share for our dinner. I felt disappointed because without the beers and cigarettes, we could have got a lot more groceries.

"What about tomorrow's meals?" I asked him.

"Don't worry about tomorrow. Enjoy today." That seemed to be his motto. He never worried about the next day.

When we had finished our chips, he produced a big bag of penny sweets to share out. Just like his parents, he had to spend every last penny. After their sweets and teeth cleaning, I settled the children into their sleeping bags. Jim was soon asleep too after finishing his beers. I was relieved that there was no repetition of the night before, although I felt we'd had enough trauma for that day already.

The next morning, the children woke early, and we had some Weetabix for our breakfast. Afterwards, they played and ran around the campsite while I washed the bowls and tidied up. Jim didn't wake up until near lunchtime. I had been wondering what we would have for lunch and dinner, because there didn't seem to be any food provisions now, and Roy wasn't due to pick us back up until late afternoon. I asked Jim what we would have for lunch and dinner, but he just shrugged.

After a mug of tea, brewed on the little stove, he went off to "sort it", whatever that meant.

I soon found out. He'd been to the phone box and rung Roy to ask him to pick us up earlier than planned. Meanwhile, I gave the children another bowl of Weetabix for their lunch. They grumbled a bit, but they knew that if they didn't eat it, there would be nothing else until they got home.

A couple of hours later, Roy arrived in his car and trailer. We packed everything in it before Roy drove us all off the campsite and onto the road, then he and Jim started to laugh and guffaw loudly. I asked what the joke was and what I had missed.

"You've got away without paying for your pitch!" Roy laughed. I didn't laugh back. He and Jim laughed and made jokes about it all the way home.

That wasn't the only time we went away in our tent. Jim promised we'd go away for a proper week's holiday in the children's school holidays, which were approaching. I gave my notice to the cleaning company as I would need to be at home for the children for the six weeks of the holidays. For some reason, Jim gave in his notice too. He said it was so that we could go on the promised holiday. Why he couldn't have just booked a week off, I have no idea.

Again, he arranged for Roy to drive us, this time to Hastings, and Moira agreed to look after our Boots again. Little Mark had asked if we could take the cat with us, but we explained that it wasn't an option.

My parents surprised us by saying they would drive down to Hastings too for the weekend. They had a Morris Traveller now with a tent attachment for the back. Usually, they avoided Jim like the plague as they both hated him, and the feeling was mutual, but they said they'd like to spend some time with their grandchildren at the seaside, so they put their feelings aside for the weekend.

Roy drove us there, and by the time my parents arrived, our tent was all set up. After they'd got their pitch, we set off to find a fish and chip shop—always a must at the seaside.

After lunch, we spent the afternoon on the beach. My mother was a keen swimmer, and once she was in the water, she gave her usual shout, which I remembered from our childhood holidays.

"Come on in! It's lovely!"

And in we went. I had a little swim with my mother while the children paddled with their grandad and found some shells and stones to put in the buckets that my parents had brought for them to play with. Jim sat on the beach watching our belongings and reading the *Daily Mail* that my father had brought with him.

When we came back up the beach, Jim took it as his cue to go off to the pub for a couple of hours. He'd done his bit, he said.

Then, as the sun went down, we returned to our respective tents and didn't see each other until the next day. Jim warmed some tins of soup, and I buttered some bread to fill us up for our tea. We had a nice peaceful night afterwards, reading by lamplight while the children slept until we were ready to sleep as well.

My parents were going home the next day, and the arrangement was that we'd do our own thing through the morning then meet back at the campsite in the afternoon to say goodbye. I think one day of Jim was enough for my parents, and one day of my parents was enough for Jim.

We set off with the children, after our breakfast, along a clifftop walk to look for a nice section of beach to go down to. After we'd been going for about twenty minutes, Jim said, "Don't look behind you."

I thought he must have spotted my parents following us, but when someone says, "Don't look behind you," well, instinctively you do.

And there, mincing along close behind us, was a naked man just in a pair of flipflops, with a sports bag slung casually over his shoulder! He'd actually passed us earlier, fully clothed, so presumably, he'd got undressed in the bushes somewhere along the way. As he went past us again, the children got the giggles and tried to imitate his walk. We, in turn, tried to hush them up.

Farther along, we spotted a lovely little bay at the bottom of the cliff. It looked like a nice, family-friendly beach, with people swimming and playing in the water, picnic blankets set out and a few windbreakers set up, so we found some steps leading down from the cliff.

As we got nearer to the beach, we stopped in surprise. Nobody was wearing any clothes, and we were about to join them! Oh, no we weren't. We turned around, went back up the steps, and found another bay a bit farther along.

When we met up with my parents later on, they did laugh at our tale of the nudist beach we nearly ended up on, and the children did their best to show their grandparents how the naked man was mincing along! We waved my parents off through the afternoon and carried on our holiday without them. I think Jim was relieved; he'd been on his best behaviour while my parents were there.

Sadly, the next couple of days went the same way as our previous camping trip, with Jim pulling me about outside the tent after the children had gone to bed. At one point, I thought he was going to push me over the cliff at the edge of the campsite, then he took all my clothes off me and I had to run back to the tent naked.

The next night, he pushed me down into some stinging nettles, and at the same time, my head cracked against something. Probably a stone. I yelled out with the pain, but he ignored me and roughly forced himself onto me. Afterwards I itched so much from the nettles and my head was bleeding and hurting a lot. Back at the tent, I poured cold water over my itching legs and got one of the children's little vests to hold against my bleeding head. I tried to tie it round with Scott's little belt so that hopefully it would stay in place while I slept.

By the Tuesday, we had run out of money and provisions, so Jim phoned Roy and arranged for him to collect us later that day. If I'd had my family allowance book with me, I could have cashed the week's money that day as it was due on Tuesdays, and that would have got us some more provisions. But Jim had given the book to Roy and signed the payment over to him before we went away to cover petrol costs.

Once we were back home, Roy had his own bright idea. He asked if he could borrow the tent to take Moira and little Danny away on holiday. In turn, Jim agreed to feed his fish and his lizard while they were gone.

So they went away the following Saturday, and Jim did his pet-feeding duties. One evening when he went round to feed them, I went with him to see how much the lizard had grown since they'd bought him. While I was there, curiosity got the better of me and I peeped into Roy's darkroom. I couldn't believe my eyes. There, pinned on the walls, were photos of me, the ones I'd never even seen, the most intimate photos that Jim had taken that awful night. I ripped them all down and tore them up straight away. I was horrified to have seen them there. Jim wouldn't comment on it. No explanation, no apology. But nothing would have been enough. The damage was done.

The following weekend, Roy and his family returned from their holiday. Little Danny had thoroughly enjoyed himself and couldn't wait to come in and play with my three and tell them all about it. Meanwhile,

Jim made three mugs of tea and took them in the garden to share with Roy and Moira. I wouldn't leave the house. I just couldn't face them after what I'd discovered that week.

Jim told me that Roy had offered to look after the tent for us, as we didn't have anywhere to store it out of the way. "He's a good bloke," Jim told me. But within two weeks, apparently, the tent had been stolen from Roy's trailer. At least that's what Jim told me. I wasn't sure what to believe as the pair of them were liars anyway. We never got the tent back, or any recompense for it.

I did feel sad when I thought of all the money we'd paid for it and now it was gone. But at the same time, I was glad because the times we'd had away in it had been unbearable. But so much worse than that was the humiliation of finding the photos in Roy's darkroom. Nothing was ever said about it by either Jim or Roy. It was as if my feelings were totally irrelevant. Just a nothing person. And I didn't know how to change that.

CHAPTER 18

Jonno

IT WAS ALWAYS VERY DIFFICULT to manage when neither of us was working. Mainly because Jim never gave me any of his dole money, so I had to do my best to feed the children from the week's family allowance, which wasn't a lot. Then some weeks he would take the family allowance book and cash it himself, then accuse me of losing it when I couldn't find it. Those weeks were the hardest, and the following week when the book was back where I kept it, he'd deny all knowledge of it supposedly going missing the week before. I was losing the plot, he'd tell me. Well, I was to a certain extent, thanks to him.

When my mother was visiting one Tuesday and discovered I was spending the family allowance on food, she was horrified. "You can't do that, Hilary," she said. "It's the children's money for things they need—like clothes, shoes, and other necessities."

"It *is* for what they need, Mum," I replied. "They need food."

She did love her grandchildren and often bought them clothes, albeit from jumble sales, which she loved, and sometimes she even bought them brand-new shoes, so I was very grateful for her help.

I did manage to find another little job. I worked for a company called Dee Minor and sold children's clothes via house parties. I was supplied with a stock of clothes and a clothes rail and had to drum up parties in friends' homes to show the goods and take orders. I worked on commission, which meant I would gradually pay for the stock as well as earn something.

I managed to get a couple of parties organised and hoped for more, by recommendation. The first one was in Lewisham, a bus ride away, so I headed off with my case full of children's clothes, and the rail, which was strapped up with a belt. The case was heavy, the rail was awkward, and my handbag, slung over my shoulder, kept slipping off. It was like a juggling act paying my fare on the bus. But worse was to come.

When the bus reached my destination, I went to get off and the case burst open, with children's clothes scattered over the floor of the bus and out onto the pavement! I realised that for this job, one really needed a car.

My next party was at Moira's sister Ria's house in Dartford, and Moira drove me there. I was happy to go with her. She was a nice woman, and I knew she put up with a lot from Roy, even though she had never said. I took a lot of orders that evening, so that gave me a boost. I told all the mums when the money had to be in by and that it was to be paid to Ria, as host of the party. Then Moira would drive me over to collect the money and deliver the clothes that had been ordered, for Ria to give out to the party guests. Only the money didn't come in on time.

I told my supervisor that I hadn't got the money in yet, and she said she would take the orders over and collect the money for me. However, she did something that I'd had strict instructions not to do. She left the clothes with Ria even though she still hadn't got the money. Then my supervisor told me it was down to me to collect the money as soon as possible. But the money was never forthcoming, even though the clothes had been given out. So I lost that job. I wasn't altogether sorry.

Someone who figured largely in our lives during our time in Sidcup was Jonno. Jim had first met him while they were both working on the buses, but it was just a fill-in job for Jonno as he was actually a qualified painter and decorator. Once he was back at his proper job, every now and then he would give Jim a bit of work too, after he'd lost his job on the buses.

He was a good few years older than us and was married with three children a bit older than our three. His wife, Margo, was a bit older than me and seemed lovely, but Jonno wasn't content with what he had.

He would often turn up at our house with some girl on his arm, and not always the same one. He would generally have a bottle of scotch on him that he'd started, and he'd give the rest to Jim in return for the use of our bed. I was disgusted at this, but whenever I protested, I was shouted down by them both and laughed at for being a prude. I also risked a good hiding later on.

When they came back downstairs, Jonno would drive his lady friend home then come back with some beers to share with Jim. After a long drinking session, he would say to my husband, "I need to go home now but don't feel like driving. Jim, will you drive me back?"

I didn't realise it at the time, but Jim didn't even have a driving licence, but he'd still get in Jonno's car and drive him the fifteen miles or so back to his home in Darenth. Then they'd have another drinking session there until Jim in turn said, "I need to go home now."

And Jonno would duly drive him back to ours, where they would have yet another drinking session. This could go on three or four times a night, with them driving each other back and forth between houses with beers aplenty, and more than once a week. I don't know how either of them was in a fit state to go to work the next day, but I did realise that Jonno must be an alcoholic.

Jim told me a few funny stories of working with Jonno. One time he was up a ladder painting a shop front when a little boy came running up and grabbed the ladder, shaking it and calling, "Hello, Mr Painter."

Fortunately, the boy's mother came and pulled him away before there was a disaster!

Apparently, though not while Jim was working with him, Jonno had once fallen from his ladder, feet first, and broken a lot of bones in his feet. Healing took a long time, but he did get back to work eventually.

One day when he'd dropped Jim back home after work, our neighbour Roy came rushing over to him with a huge smile on his face. He told him excitedly about some scam he'd been up to and that he'd made about fifty quid from it.

"Good for you," Jim said as Roy scuttled back down his own front path.

As Jim turned to come in, he spotted something on the floor. He picked it up and came quickly indoors. It was fifty pounds in five-pound notes, all rolled up in an elastic band.

"We've come into some luck," Jim said to me. "We're going out tonight."

A few minutes after that, we heard Roy shouting for Jim over the back fence, so he went out to see him.

"You know that fifty quid I got?" he said. "I've only gone and dropped it somewhere."

When Jim came back in and told me, I tried to get him to give it back, but he wouldn't. He said it wasn't honestly come by so he didn't feel bad about it. Then he told me to get ready because we were going out for a meal. I didn't want to go out on dishonest money, I didn't want to go out at all, but I didn't have a choice. We put the children to bed and Jim went to get the babysitter while I got changed. He always laid out on the bed my clothes that he wanted me to wear. I hated that, as although they were my clothes, he didn't match them up in the way that I would have. He didn't ask our usual neighbour to babysit though. He actually asked Roy! Talk about rubbing salt into a wound.

It wasn't a pleasant evening. The meal itself was very nice. We went to a Chinese restaurant at the top of town. But any time we went out together, I would dread how the evening would end. This time was no different. After our meal, Jim said we'd go the back way home. That was via a huge, grassy hill running between the town and the hospital, down towards where we lived at the bottom end of the hill. It was pitch-black on the hill and a favourite place for Jim to take me, away from everyone and everything.

As soon as we got onto the grass, Jim pulled my legs away, and as I fell, he leapt on top of me. This was still embarrassingly close to the road and the houses there. I struggled to get away, but Jim kept lashing out at me and kicking my legs away, bringing me to the ground again. Then he put his hands around my throat. As soon as I managed to break free, I started to scream as loudly as I could, but he still wouldn't leave me alone. Quite quickly a police car pulled up. Two officers got out, came, and questioned us. As soon as they realised that we were husband and wife, they didn't want to know. They told us we should go home then they got back in their car and drove off.

Jim put his arm around me and started walking me down the hill towards home. But he still kept stopping and pulling me about like a rag doll. Then he wanted me to walk in front of him and wet myself. I hated doing that and refused, but he wasn't going to give up. He kept stopping and kissing me, touching me, and tickling me to try to make me go. I felt cold and miserable and just wanted to get home. After about half an hour of this, I did wet myself just to get the whole thing over and done with. But once I had done that, he pulled off my wet tights and panties and even my skirt. Then he attempted to have sex with me, which took absolutely ages. Afterwards he walked me down the rest of the hill with no skirt on, just in a pretty blouse that hardly covered anything below my waist. When we came out of the field, I had to walk along the road like it for about five minutes to our house.

I ran straight up to our bedroom the minute we got in, while Jim sent Roy home and thanked him for babysitting. Then he came up to the bedroom and started all over again wanting sex. I was just so tired; it must have taken us nearly two hours to come down that hill. A walk that should only take about fifteen minutes.

The next day after work, Jim told me that he and Jonno were going to go away for a week together, in a caravan somewhere. I forget where. I was most surprised. After all, who went away with their workmate/boss, leaving their wives and families at home? Well, Jim and Jonno did. I felt rather put out at first, thinking, *What about us?* Then I remembered our disastrous camping trips and felt glad we weren't all invited. In fact, the children and I had a lovely stress-free week. One day I took them over to the Footscray Meadows, where we had a picnic and played a simple game of cricket. The day before they were due back, I made a cake with the children, to welcome their dad home. We iced it and decorated it with lots of sugar flowers on top.

The pair of them arrived back through the afternoon the next day and came in with a big carrier bag full of beers, so that was their evening sorted. The children brought the cake out, but their dad said to save it for tomorrow.

"We made it for you, Daddy," Melissa told him. "You have to have some."

But he still said he'd have some the next day, so disappointed, they took the cake back to the kitchen. I let them have a small slice each before they went to bed. I went to bed early too, as Jim and Jonno were having a drinking session for the evening. Jim had already driven Jonno home, had some beers there, and then Jonno had driven him back again, and they were in our living room drinking more beers. I heard them come and go a couple of times before I fell asleep. It was laughable how they would come and go all night like that! It was just a good job the next day was a Sunday.

About a week after their holiday, Jonno came round with a big packet of photographs from their week away. I was very eager to see them, but Jim would not let me. I just briefly saw the top photo, which was of Jim, presumably in the caravan, crouched on the floor wearing just a ladies' frilly apron. No explanation was given.

A few weeks later, Jonno invited us both to a party at his home. I'd completely gone off going to parties with my husband by this time, but there was no getting out of it. Jonno offered us to stay over, so we organised our babysitter, who was happy to stay the night at ours. When the day came, Jonno picked us up early evening and drove us back to his. Jim ignored me for most of the evening and spent it laughing, joking, and drinking the night away with Jonno's male friends. I didn't know anyone else there apart from Jonno's wife, Margo, who I didn't know well anyway, but she was busy playing hostess. Being shy and not really a drinker, I just sat on a chair in a corner all evening like the "nothing person" I felt I was.

Halfway through the evening, I asked Margo where the bathroom was, and she directed me upstairs. Jim must have heard me asking and dashed up the stairs after me, pushing past me and barring my way to the toilet. He wanted me to wet myself there on the upstairs landing carpet. So I said that I didn't need to go after all, but then he barred my way from going back down the stairs. He must have kept me up there for about half an hour, drunkenly slobbering over me, kissing, cuddling, and tickling me until I could hold it in no longer and wet myself there on the landing. I felt awful doing that in someone else's house. Jim pulled off my wet tights and panties, rolled them up, and put them in his pocket, then to my surprise, he pulled my dress off as well. Next, he forced me to run up and down the landing in just my bra. I was terrified that someone would look up and see me, or come upstairs even to use the bathroom, but fortunately, nobody did. I'd tried my hardest not to cry or make any noise while we were up there, so no one would be alerted.

Eventually, he gave me back my dress and we went downstairs, where Jonno gave Jim a huge grin and a thumbs up. I wondered if he'd seen.

I found another out-of-the-way chair and sat there for the rest of the evening, feeling very uncomfortable with no tights and panties on under my dress.

Gradually, after midnight, the guests started to leave, and Margo went up to bed. After the last one had gone, Jonno brought us some cushions and blankets to make up a bed for ourselves on the living room floor. I couldn't wait to lie down and shut my eyes, and I climbed into the make-shift bed, still with my dress on. I was so tired. Jim wasn't having that though. He pulled all the blankets off me and then removed my dress. After that, he started mauling me about in his drunken state and wouldn't let me pull the blankets back.

Within a few minutes, Jonno came downstairs and into the room, wearing just his boxer shorts. To my horror, he started stroking me and touching me intimately, and my husband didn't even seem to mind! I wondered if it had been planned. I couldn't bear the feel of Jonno's hard, rough hands on me but tried my best to stay silent so as not to wake his wife or children. It seemed to go on for a long time, and the two of them easily overpowered me.

At last, after sitting and having another beer with Jim, next to my practically naked body, Jonno went back upstairs, hopefully to bed. Although I still had no blankets on, I pretended to have fallen asleep while they had been drinking, in the hopes of being left alone. Then Jim got up and went into the kitchen. I thought probably to get another beer, but seconds later, he came back in holding a huge carving knife. This was my end, I thought, as he came at me with it.

I didn't know if he saw me peep, but I was too exhausted physically and emotionally to run or fight and just shut my eyes and waited for the impact. Barely seconds later, it came. There was a massive thud on my chest and my eyes opened in shock. There was no blood. He must have brought the handle of the knife down on me. I cannot remember anything after that, although I knew I hadn't been properly stabbed as there was no blood, just a huge bruise—and as ever, no apology or explanation in the morning. Or any time after.

Jonno dutifully drove us home the next morning. The minute I got in, I ran myself a bath and put fresh clothes on, hoping it would help me feel better. It didn't.

The two men spent the day drinking and driving each other backwards and forwards as was their want. Jonno didn't apologise to me either. Just how insignificant a person was I?

Some weeks later, we received a letter from the Council saying we were shortly going to be evicted. I was devastated. Especially when I remembered our housing officer, Jane Templer, praising me, when Jim had been in prison, because the rent arrears were nearly all paid up.

"Don't worry. I'll sort it" was all Jim said when he saw how upset I was. His stock answer to everything.

CHAPTER 19

Another New Start

UNBEKNOWN TO ME, THE DAY of eviction had arrived. I'd taken the children to school as usual, but when I got back, my front door was open and there was a removal van outside. My heart sank. Jim was talking to Roy and Moira in their front garden, telling them the situation. They had kindly offered to pick our little ones up from school along with Danny later. The removal men apparently had waited for me to get back from the school, then they informed us that we weren't allowed to stay in the property while they went about their business, but they did give me ten minutes to grab anything important that I needed. They also told us to get ourselves up to the Council offices in Bexleyheath.

The house was not tidy. Nothing had been packed up because Jim had assured me it wouldn't happen. The breakfast things were still on the table, wet washing was in the bath, and the beds were still unmade. Embarrassing! But nothing could be done about that. In the ten minutes, I made sure I had my purse, my family allowance book, and my make-up bag. Then we left the house for the last time and went across the road to get the bus to the Council offices.

It was heartbreaking standing at the bus stop watching all our belongings being loaded into the van and having absolutely no idea where they were taking them. When the bus came, the conductor recognised Jim from his time on the buses.

"Looks like someone's moving," he said, nodding across to the van.

"Yes, us," replied Jim. Fortunately, the conductor was too busy to give us time to enlarge on that.

When we arrived at the Council offices, they kept us waiting for two hours before anyone would see us, then we were told to come back at four o'clock.

I was so worried, wondering if we would be back in bed and breakfast. Or worse, would they refuse to help us now? I was also worried about the children and what Roy and Moira would tell them. But as ever, Jim kept telling me not to worry. We went and got a coffee and a sandwich and sat on a bench with them, watching all the shoppers just to kill time. It didn't stop me worrying though.

We went back to the offices at four, and this time we were seen straight away. We were given an address in Peckham where we could go with our children. No explanation as to what sort of place it was. A bed and breakfast? Shared house? We were given a door key, so that was a good sign.

We got the bus back to Sidcup straight away, to collect the children, and when we got to Roy and Moira's, they were happily eating corned beef sandwiches with Danny, and Roy and Moira were grinning at us.

"We know exactly where you're going!" Roy exclaimed.

"How? Where?" we chorused.

"You're going to a lovely Victorian-style house in Peckham." Roy laughed. "We followed the van with your stuff in!"

We all laughed then. It was a relief really to know exactly where we were going, and Roy said he'd drive us there, so that was an added bonus.

What did make me sad though was that I hadn't had a chance to say goodbye to my friends in the Bible group. Much as I loved the group, none of them knew how things really were for me, and they probably would have been shocked to know we'd been evicted.

Anyway, a new start had to be made and had to be better, hopefully. Away from Jonno was especially good, though I didn't voice that to Jim. And as much as I was grateful to Roy for driving us to our new home, I was also glad to get away from him, although he did say he would try to catch our cat Boots and drive him over to us as well when he could. I was sad that we hadn't been able to find Boots before we'd set off earlier in the car. But after our move, we lost contact with Roy and Moira, and I never had the money to travel back to Sidcup to look for Boots myself.

My mother said we were very cruel to have left our cat behind. I couldn't tell her the circumstances of our move, so she just didn't understand.

The house itself was a big, three-bedroom house and in better condition than the Sidcup one. Jane Templer from the Council came to see us during that first week and explained that this was still a temporary accommodation and we'd have to get our rent arrears completely cleared before we could move back to Kent or be considered for a permanent Council house.

For all the worrying about the children, they were actually quite happy with everything and thought it was all a big adventure! We got them into a nearby primary school, a five-minute walk away, as opposed to the forty-minute walk they'd had in Sidcup. They soon settled in and made some new friends.

After a couple of weeks, I realised that a few things had been left behind in the Sidcup house. There were some important papers, bills, recipes, poems, and writing I had done, and letters that would have been in the cupboard under the stairs. I felt sad because I knew we would never get them back now, and it was the second time I had lost things that were important to me.

We made friends with the young couple next door to us, Mick and Angie. They had no children of their own but offered to babysit for us any time. We took them up on their offer the next week, as there was a pub on the corner of our road and it had advertised a fancy-dress night. We both loved fancy dress. Jim put on his court jester outfit that he'd hired for a mate's stag do a couple of years previously but had never taken back. I dressed as a pixie, in an outfit I had put together myself. However, when we got to the pub, absolutely no one else was dressed up, apart from the barmaid, who was dressed as Nell Gwyn. It was the first time we'd been in the pub, and everyone just looked at us oddly. So after our first drink, we went home, got changed into our regular going-out clothes, and went off to another pub, where Jim made one or two friends.

Early one evening, after the children had gone to bed, Mick and Angie were in our front room with us, the boys having a beer, and Angie and I a cup of coffee. We watched a shabbily dressed man staggering along the pavement past our window. We giggled at him, but then he staggered back and plonked himself on our front wall.

"Tell him to clear off!" said Mick.

"He's not doing any harm. He's probably drunk," I replied, not wanting any fuss.

We ignored him for a bit, until he suddenly rolled off the wall and into our front garden.

"Definitely drunk!" Jim declared as he pulled the curtains closed. "He'll be gone in the morning when he's sobered up."

"I'm going out to see if he's all right," Angie put in. She was a registered nurse, and her nursing instincts had kicked in. "I think he might be ill."

"He's drunk!" the boys chorused, laughing.

Angie went out, telling us to be prepared to run to the phone box to call for an ambulance. She was very quickly back in.

"He's drunk," she stated as she sat down with her coffee. And yes, he was gone by the next morning.

I thought it might be useful having a nurse as a next-door neighbour. You never knew what might happen with a family.

Quite by chance, during our first week there, I met up with a family who lived in the next road, who were from the local Bible group. They became good friends of mine and showed me where the group met together in New Cross. I started going regularly and made some more friends there, though I still kept my private life private from them. It was a long way to go to their meetings, and my friends round the corner couldn't fit us in their car, but I was quite happy to go on the bus with the children.

I got a job quite quickly as a PA in a small, local company. I really enjoyed the job. It was at that time that I discovered Pot Noodles, probably new on the market then, and I would very often buy one for my lunch and make it up in the office kitchen.

After I'd been there for a couple of months, I found I was expecting another baby. I must have fallen pregnant shortly before we had left Sidcup.

As I got nearer to my due date, I started to work four days a week as opposed to my usual full week. It gave me a chance to get things ready for my new baby, while the children were at school.

About ten days before my baby was due, I left work after lunch to go for my routine midwife appointment. I felt fine, but she told me my blood pressure was very high and I should go home and put my feet up. I could do that because it was the school holidays and Jim had taken the children to London Zoo for the day, so I came home to a nice, quiet house.

I hadn't been home long when I started to get the familiar pains, which I knew could only mean one thing. I started to get a bit anxious for my family's return as the afternoon wore on. I had no way of contacting them. They didn't get home until about seven o'clock, and as soon as they came through the front door, happy and laughing, I burst out that I was in labour.

"Well, the kids have worn me out. I must have a lie down before I do anything else" was Jim's reply, and he promptly went upstairs to bed.

The children had already eaten, so I managed to get them off to bed, after they'd told me a bit about the animals, and we'd talked about the new baby on its way, and guessed whether it would be a boy or a girl, in between my labour pains. They were all so excited! But I was still anxious and dreading Jim's reaction if I had to wake him up, which I felt sure I would.

Fortunately, he came downstairs of his own accord, while I was bracing myself to scramble up the stairs to wake him. He got Mick and Angie in to babysit then ran round the corner to see a mate who'd already offered to drive us to hospital in his van, when the time came. Now was the time, and they came back for me and drove us to the hospital.

I was hardly in the hospital any length of time when I gave birth to another beautiful baby boy, and we called him Micah.

The following morning, Jim phoned my job to tell them I wouldn't be coming in that day.

"It's OK," my boss said. "She doesn't come in on Wednesdays."

"Well, she won't be in Thursday, Friday, or after that. She's had the baby!" He laughed.

It had already been agreed that I would leave the job altogether when my baby arrived.

I was only in the hospital for a couple of days with baby Micah. He was quite a big baby, chubbier than the others had been, and we could see from the start that he was going to be a redhead. While I was still in hospital, I received some lovely flowers in a blue train engine planter that was delivered to the hospital. I'd always wanted one, and this one had been sent by my boss. A little flag in the arrangement said, "Congratulations," and a note was enclosed wishing me all the best and thanking me for the work I had done. It made me so happy—not just the cute flower arrangement but for the words of appreciation too.

Once home, we soon settled into a routine. The children were thrilled with their little brother, and I don't think any baby could have had more fuss made of him. He never cried. If he looked like he was going to, there was always someone to make a fuss of him. I could see him being spoilt!

Micah was only a few weeks old when I contracted scarlet fever and stayed in bed feeling very poorly and covered in a bright red rash. Surprisingly, no one else in the house caught it, even though it was generally considered to be a child's illness, and I was still able to breastfeed little Micah without him even catching it.

After a few months, we had to move again. Still in Peckham, still temporary, and still a five-minute walk from the children's school, just in the opposite direction. I still went to the same Bible group in New Cross, but now we had to walk because I wasn't working so didn't have the bus fare. Also, I only had a big pram that couldn't go on the bus anyway, so we walked it every week with Micah in the pram and the children either side. It took us an hour and a half each way, but we were young and fit, and my friends were there, so it was worth the walk.

It was a very quiet street that we moved to, with a few other families in, and the children soon made friends with them. When it was time for all the children to come home from school, I'd stand at the gate with little Micah in my arms, and as the children started to appear round the corner, whether they were mine or the neighbours', he would have the biggest smile on his face. I think home from school time was his favourite time of day. He was such a happy baby, and all the street's children loved him and made a fuss of him.

My Melissa took a little girl called Mary under her wing while we were living there. She was a tiny, thin, little girl, aged about 4, and didn't seem to be very well looked after. Mary was always hungry, her long hair unbrushed, and she never seemed to have enough clothes on. And that's where Melissa's ever-present mothering instinct came in.

We watched Mary gradually become a happy, little girl with all Melissa's love and attention. Although my Mark was a couple of years older than her, Melissa would sort through his clothes to find things he had grown out of or didn't wear anymore, such as T-shirts, vests, jumpers, shorts, and socks, and dressed Mary to keep her warm. She even sorted out a little jacket that Mark had grown out of as well. She'd wash her and brush her hair, putting pretty clips in it, and tell her she was a princess. Melissa would also beg me to do dinner for Mary, and sometimes she would make her some toast as she had never had any breakfast. If we went to the park, Melissa would bring Mary too. The only thing she didn't do was sleep at ours.

After we moved there, Jim got a job driving and delivering furniture to the various McDonald's venues around London. On a Saturday, he would sometimes take our older children in the van with him, and they got spoilt with burgers and milkshakes from some of the stores. I'd sometimes get a burger brought back for me as well. I think it was the only time in our marriage where we'd been able to afford McDonald's for our children!

Another good memory I have from our time in Peckham is the children's school sports day. This was held in a nearby park as there were no grass areas or playing fields in the London schools back then. I took Micah along in his pram. I knew he'd love seeing all the children running and jumping.

I shouted and cheered for Melissa, Scott, and Mark, and they all did well. I was proud of my children whatever they did and whether they came first or last. At the end of the day, a parents' race was announced. I'd always been good at running and thought I'd have a go. A little part of me thought that if I won, other mums would congratulate me and I could make some local friends that way.

I asked a mum who wasn't racing to watch baby Micah, then I hurried over to the starting line, along with another dozen or so mums and dads. I was feeling quite confident, although a couple of the dads looked like they might be quite athletic.

"We're going to do something different this year," the headteacher said into the tannoy. "We're going to have a skipping race." And skipping ropes were given out to us all.

Now normally that wouldn't have been a problem, but on this particular day, I was wearing a long, flowing, hippy-style skirt that was my preferred style of dress. There was no way I could hitch it up enough to skip, and I think I was the last one to set off and the last one to reach the end! No cheers or congratulations for me after all, except when I took back charge of baby Micah and he just beamed at me happily. He didn't care if I won or lost.

This disastrous experience inspired me to write the following poem—embellished rather for effect but loosely based on that race:

Sports Day

> I went to school for the children's sports,
> Wearing my new Bermuda shorts,
> Waiting for the race for mums
> So I could well impress my chums,
> From whom (they're being out of condition)
> I felt there was no competition.
> We watched our offspring jump and run
> And watched the darlings having fun,
> Cheering on our little dears.
> While me—I knew I had no fears.
> When they called out, "All mums and dads!"
> I proudly waved to my small lads,
> Knowing my athletic skill,
> Bermuda shorts, and iron will
> Would make me champion of them all—
> The fastest parent in the school.
> I could hear my sons proclaiming, "Yes!
> We always knew our mum was best!"
> So as we lined up for our race,
> I hitched my shorts up round my waist,
> And feeling I'd already won,
> I ran as I had never run.
> Then came the dreadful ripping sound,
> And as my shorts fell to the ground,

> I felt a draught on my behind.
> Fate that day was quite unkind.
> My ego certainly took a blast.
> Instead of first, I came in last.
> So the moral of this tale, you see,
> Is (take a lesson here from me)
> Before you enter any sports,
> Remember: always check your shorts.

A little fun verse. Something I often did was to put pen to paper!

Jim had missed their sports day due to his driving job, but he had his own keep-fit regime. Every day, early evening, he would put on his sports vest, shorts, and trainers that he'd bought recently from a trip to Walworth Road and go jogging around the block. The children waited for him at the gate with bottles of water. One for him to drink when he got back and the others to pour over him to cool him down. I don't know who enjoyed it more: Jim or the children.

He always said that he felt so much better after his run, so one day I said I'd go with him. I donned some slacks, a T-shirt, and flat shoes that I could run in (no luxury sports gear for me), and we set off together, leaving the children at the gate with their bottles of water. They had strict instructions not to pour them over me when we got back, and little Micah was outside with them, strapped in his pram.

We'd hardly gone any distance when Jim started jogging faster, ahead of me.

"Hey, wait for me!" I called.

"I can't! We have to go at our own pace, and this is mine!" he called back.

I felt a bit disappointed at that. I could've run and kept up with him, but it was supposed to be jogging so I carried on at my own pace and watched him disappear round the corner. When I rounded that corner, he'd obviously gone round the next one as well. Across the road from me were some young lads putting their snooker cues into their car. As I drew level with them, they started catcalling and wolf-whistling, and one of them shouted, "Hey! If you streak, we'll streak with you!"

I yelled out "Jim! *Jim!*" But no reply came. I was a little bit worried about these lads at the time, though I'm sure now they just meant it as harmless fun. When I got back home, Jim had been back and had even had a quick shower already. I didn't go jogging anymore after that.

There was another group of lads that we got to know at that time. The ringleader was Vince. He and his pals were always tinkering about with cars outside our house. That was because his uncle Geordie, who lived a few doors down from us, had a large motorhome parked outside his house, so when Vince visited his uncle, he would park nearby, which usually meant by ours.

Jim made friends with Vince and his pals and got me making mugs of tea and sandwiches for them. He even let them in to use the toilet as it was nearer than going back to Geordie's.

We didn't really know Geordie, because he was a long-distance lorry driver and away a lot of the time. He had several children, and they went to school with ours, so of course, they were all friends.

One day Vince knocked on the door and found that I was in by myself. Straightaway, he pushed in and shoved me against the side of the hallway and started kissing me! I was quite shocked as I was probably about ten years older than him. Then he started pushing himself up against me. I tried my hardest to push him away. It could only have been a few seconds because just then, Jim's cousin Dave appeared at the door, and Vince let go and scuttled off outside. I slammed the door after him. Dave asked me if I was OK, and I assured him I was, whereupon he went into the front room and put the television on to watch the racing and wait for Jim to come home.

I never told Jim what Vince had done, because I didn't know what his reaction would be, whether he would be angry at me or if he would try to initiate something with Vince; I remembered those awful times with Jonno. I don't know if Dave ever said anything to Jim about it either, because Dave was very quiet and never said much at the best of times.

Another bad memory surfaced from when we had lived in Sidcup. Dave had come to stay over for a couple of nights, and the second night, in the early hours of the morning, Jim had forced me downstairs and tried to push me into Dave's bed that was made up on the floor. I was terrified that Dave would wake up. Fortunately, he didn't. Or if he did, he didn't let on. Was he even in on it? I had begun to doubt everything and everyone back then, but things seemed to have been a bit better since coming to Peckham, and I didn't want to rock the boat.

When the summer holidays came, our neighbour Geordie took his family off abroad for the entire six weeks in his motorhome, and he left his nephew to stay in his house and look after it. Jim was still pally with Vince, having him and his mates in sometimes to watch the football on television. I put on a show of being friendly, but if he knocked when I was in on my own, I just didn't open the door.

Around this time, several neighbours had their televisions stolen. It made me think back to when Jim had got in trouble over the televisions in Sidcup, so I was a bit worried that he'd gone back to his old ways.

One day, late afternoon, I came home from a picnic with the children and was surprised to see that my front sash window was wide open, and I knew that Jim was not at home. I told the children to keep quiet and opened the door cautiously, but as the front door creaked, I heard a man curse and then a thud. I looked in the room, and there was our television in the middle of the floor and Vince was clambering out the back window.

As soon as Jim came back, I told him and we reported it to the police. I had to make a statement, but I was a bit worried about it as I was the only person who could identify Vince, and of course, I had to give them his uncle Geordie's address as I knew he was staying there throughout the summer holidays. Having said that, I was relieved to know that the stolen televisions were nothing to do with Jim after all and that ours hadn't actually been taken either.

I tried to put it out of my mind and carry on with my day-to-day activities. I'd started doing an early morning cleaning job as Jim was no longer working for McDonald's and money was really tight. I'd leave the house at about six in the morning and be back again soon after eight-thirty. This worked well because it meant the children wouldn't even miss me.

One morning on my way to work, I heard a car approaching behind me. Generally, there was hardly any traffic at that time of the morning. It sounded like it was really revving up, and it then mounted the pavement and sped past me with barely inches to spare! It was Vince. And it happened three mornings running. I left the job that week because I was so frightened by this.

Then one Saturday morning, Jim and I went shopping with the children. We had only been gone a few minutes and had turned the first corner when Vince came driving at all of us, skidding dangerously close, past the pram. He must have watched us all leave our house. We were just relieved that his uncle Geordie and family were due back from their holiday in a few days. It actually happened again a couple of days later, and I wouldn't leave the house after that. But at least our neighbour would be back over the weekend. And presumably Vince would go back to his own home, wherever that was.

We couldn't have been more relieved when we saw Geordie's motorhome back outside his house and we relaxed a bit at last.

Until a couple of nights later, when we were all upstairs in bed and heard a loud banging on our front door. Jim got up, grabbed his dressing gown, and went down to see who it was. I stood at the top of the stairs out of curiosity.

It was Geordie. "How dare you bring the police to my door when I'm not there?" he demanded, pushing his way in. He kept pushing Jim along the hallway and up the stairs. The children were crying on the landing, having been woken by the shouting, and little Micah was howling in his cot. Although Jim was six feet tall, he was no match for Geordie, who was very broad and built like an ox and kept pushing Jim and shouting until they were at the top of the stairs. Then Geordie whipped out a knife, which flashed in the semi-darkness as he lunged at Jim with it. He then went back downstairs and out of the front door, slamming it violently behind him.

The whole thing could only have lasted a matter of seconds, but we were all traumatised by this encounter. The knife had connected with Jim's left shoulder through his dressing gown, so I pulled myself together and washed the blood from his shoulder and plastered it up the best I could. In the morning, he took himself off to the hospital, where they stitched it properly. It would have been a lot worse if it hadn't been for his thick towelling dressing gown.

When Jim returned from the hospital, duly patched up, the children made a huge fuss of him and had made a cake for him. That same day, he telephoned Jane Templer at the Council offices and told her what had been happening. She was very sympathetic but said we couldn't expect to be moved elsewhere until our arrears were paid in full, whereupon we could come back to Kent.

We were sad to hear that as we still had a lot of arrears and had guessed that would be the case. However, a few days later, Jane came up to Peckham to see us. She said again that we shouldn't really be moved until our arrears were paid up, but she said she'd see what she could do.

True to her word, she contacted us a couple of weeks later, telling us we could move into a house in Erith. It was small, she said, and still temporary housing, but it would get us out of London and back into Kent.

"Yes, please!" we both said.

CHAPTER 20

Out of London

IT WAS A DEAR, LITTLE house in Erith that we moved into. It was in a row of houses that all used to be shops, so the front door opened directly onto the street from our living room, which had a huge window facing the street. The kitchen and bathroom were off the living room, and upstairs were two average-sized bedrooms and a tiny box room off one of them.

The back garden was quite big, and behind the street's gardens was a huge landing area that was used for helicopters coming for repairs. The children loved it when this happened, and along with the neighbours' children, they would all be at their back fences, watching with excitement. We knew when a helicopter was due to land because we all had a note through the door warning us to take our washing in! A couple of times, the workmen let a few of the children come over the fence and have a closer look at the helicopters. Once they even let them take turns to sit inside, though only while it was stationary of course.

Jim and I were so happy to have got out of London, and as before, the children just thought it was all another adventure. Micah was still too little to voice a view and was still a happy and contented little boy.

I was happy as well because I knew some from the local Bible group from when I was growing up. I also knew where they met, so straight away I went and made some new friends. But because our move to Erith had been so quick and unexpected, once again I hadn't had a chance to say goodbye to my friends in the Peckham group. Also, I have often wondered since what became of little Mary.

There was a school very close by on the same road as us, and we got the children in straight away. By this time, Melissa was 11 and in her last year of primary school. After they'd been there a few weeks, the headmaster called us in to speak to him.

He said, "What's happened with your children? The three of them are very bright, but they're way behind our children here."

That made us so sad. We knew our children were bright but couldn't understand why they should be so behind in their education. After a good chat with the headmaster, and once he realised that we had come from Peckham, he said that now he understood. He explained that a lot of the schools in that area were more about keeping the children off the streets than providing education. Although it seemed really sad, we had to accept his explanation. The three of them were quite happy in their new school, so that was a positive, and hopefully they would in time catch up. As the headmaster had said, they were bright children.

I had a lot of kindness shown by my friends in the Bible group. I never discussed in depth how things were in my difficult home life, but they seemed to realise that I really struggled financially, and on a few occasions, we had a food parcel delivered anonymously. Another time I was asked if there was anything specific that I needed for the children because some money had been donated, again anonymously, to help me. I said we needed bedding and was subsequently bought four continental quilts for the children. Luxury! Back then, we just had sheets and blankets, and not enough at that. I was truly overwhelmed by this kindness, and although Jim had gone back to his mistreatment of me, I was happy with my new friends, my dear children, and baby Micah, who was a real joy. Everybody loved him.

Micah was about one and a half and I was still breastfeeding him at bedtime but felt it was now time to wean him off completely. I was taking something called the mini-pill for contraception, but I knew that was only satisfactory while breastfeeding so I went to the doctor to have a coil fitted instead.

I had noticed that I was putting on some weight, and my mother had suggested it was contentment as I was much happier out of London. Or even middle age spread come early! I did have a slight suspicion that

I could be pregnant again though and had spoken to Angie, my nurse friend from Peckham. She reassured me that it would be more than the doctor's job was worth to fit a coil into someone who was pregnant.

We had no home pregnancy kits back then, but I did say to the doctor that I thought I might be pregnant and thought he might give me a pregnancy test first just to check. But he didn't. He just said that I couldn't possibly be pregnant while taking the mini-pill and still feeding my boy. So he inserted the coil and sent me home again. All that was missing was a pat on the head!

Later that evening after the children had gone to bed, I started to feel unwell with bad stomach cramps, so I went up to bed early. I must have slept for quite a while because I wasn't aware of Jim coming to bed, but I woke up at around four o'clock in bad pain still. Jim said if I could get through until the morning, he would then get me to the doctor or hospital. I tried to hide my pain from him and I think he went back to sleep, but I'm sure I didn't. It felt almost like labour pains, and in the morning, Jim went out to the phone box, rang the doctor, and asked for a home visit. But the doctor refused. He said it sounded like my body was rejecting the coil so I would need to come to the surgery to have it removed.

"But she can't walk to get there," Jim told him.

"Well, she came here to have it put in, so she needs to come back here to have it removed" was his answer, and he still refused to come out.

Jim came home and told me what the doctor had said. We didn't have the money for a taxi, and as my pains were getting worse, he considered phoning directly for an ambulance instead. But at that moment, there was a knock on the door, and there stood Jane Templer from the Council. She took in the situation straight away and drove me straight to the doctor's surgery, while Jim stayed home with the children as it was the Easter school holidays.

When we got there, I didn't have to wait. I was helped straight into the doctor's room and onto the bed ready to have the offending coil removed.

"Am I having a miscarriage?" I asked.

He didn't answer my question. "I just need to remove this coil" was all he said, and as he went to do so, he exclaimed, "Oh my goodness!"

"I'm having a miscarriage, aren't I?" I stuttered again, but still, he would not answer.

"We need to get you to hospital straight away" was all he said. An ambulance was organised, and I was whipped off to hospital immediately.

When we got there, I was put in a bed in a room by myself. It must have been off the maternity ward because I kept hearing new baby cries. I felt very alone and frightened.

At last, someone came in. A lady in uniform with a stethoscope that she put on my stomach and listened. Then she gave it to me to listen to my baby's heartbeat.

I could hear it plainly. Now I knew! "Does this mean that I won't lose my baby after all?" I asked. No one had actually said the word "miscarriage" so I felt a bit muddled.

"I'm afraid we can't change that," she said sadly.

In that case, I just couldn't understand why she'd let me listen to this precious heartbeat.

In time, after a lot of pain, a lot of time on my own, and hearing other people's newborn babies, I gave birth to my own tiny, little boy. Apparently, I'd been five months' pregnant. He looked perfect, though barely the size of a Barbie doll. He didn't live at all outside my womb, and I went home later while my baby stayed there to be disposed of by the hospital. I called him Stephen.

The children were happy to have me back home, and later that same evening, there was a special meeting with our Bible group. Although I was feeling far from my best and couldn't even walk properly, I really wanted to go. So one of my friends from the group said she would pick me up but wouldn't have room for the children in her car. Much to my surprise, Jim said he would walk up with the children as it was only about fifteen minutes' walk away. He hadn't been to a Bible meeting with me since before we were married, so I got quite excited, wondering if at long last this would be the start of getting the old Jim back.

It was a lovely meeting, but really, I probably should have stayed back in bed or at least stayed at home with my feet up. I still felt rough and was still bleeding. When the meeting had finished and my friend came to take me back to her car, Jim said, "It's OK. She's gonna take a slow walk back with me and the kids."

Was I? I knew better than to argue with him, and it was the slowest and most painful walk I've ever done.

CHAPTER 21

Life Goes On

LIFE WENT ON IN ERITH. Jim didn't come to any more meetings with me, and he still wasn't working. I didn't feel up to getting a job just yet, so as ever, money was very tight. Melissa didn't pass the 11 plus exam but went into the top stream at the local senior school. Jim had made his mark in his new local, a pub that conveniently was just across the road from us. So that's where he was most evenings, drinking, spending our little bit of money, then drinking some more on borrowed money.

Next door to us was a young couple, Dave and Maureen. They had a little girl aged about 3, and twin girls a couple of years younger. Dave and Maureen had a lot of help from social services and various other organisations, partly to help with having twins and also because they both seemed to have learning difficulties.

Maureen was always busy with her girls, but Dave was quite eager to be friends with everyone and seemed to think that Jim was his new best mate. Anything Jim said, he would take as gospel, and he got teased mercilessly by him. But fortunately, it all went completely over his head. One day Jim told him that, along with some of the neighbours, we were into wife-swapping and if he knocked on our door at eight o'clock that evening, I would be up for it. I really grumbled at Jim about that. He said it was just a joke, but I thought it was in really bad taste.

That evening Jim took himself over the road to the pub, and on the dot of eight, there was a knock on the door. It was our neighbour, Dave.

I opened the door and he just stood and looked at me for ages. In the end, I said, "Did you want something, Dave?"

After a bit more hesitation, he mumbled, "Have you got an envelope?"

I told Jim when he came home later, and he laughed his head off! I just battered him with a scatter cushion.

Our house in Erith was really close to the River Thames, and there was a lovely river walk nearby. We often took the children along there. We could see Essex on the other side of the river and had to explain to the boys that it wasn't actually another country. Melissa teased them for a long time about that.

Jim felt that at 11, Melissa was old enough and responsible enough to watch her brothers while the two of us went out for an hour or so. I knew she was very responsible, but I wasn't happy about it and thought back to previous times when we'd been out alone. But Melissa was eager to please, and I couldn't tell her my fears, so once or twice a week Jim and I would go for one of our "romantic" walks through the evening. The mistreatment was back. I lost count of the times he pulled me over and leapt on top of me. We usually started off on the river walk, then veered off elsewhere. More than once he pushed me down in someone's front garden for sex. This was unbearable. I managed to teach myself to fall with minimal injury because we were nowhere near to the hospital now. I never told anyone about this though, and certainly not the children. I always put on a smile when we came back.

On top of this, I was still grieving for my lost baby. It didn't seem to affect Jim, but he hadn't been there to hear his little heartbeat or to see him when he was born. The doctor had offered for him to see the baby when he came to take me home, but he refused. He couldn't see the point.

Several months after losing Stephen, I found I was pregnant again, despite taking contraception. I was told by several well-meaning friends that it was a good thing and would help with the healing of my grief.

I wasn't so sure. I was actually quite worried as I didn't know how we could possibly afford another mouth to feed, especially with Jim still not working. I also worried about his rough treatment of me and if it would damage my baby, although it hadn't in the past.

My friends from the Bible group were still very kind. They knew we struggled financially. One couple took the children and me out somewhere one day for afternoon tea. It was such a huge treat, and I was so proud of my children's good behaviour and manners that day. Someone else anonymously sent me some money to buy some more bedding, ready for the baby I was expecting, and there was even enough money left over for me to buy a new maternity dress from the local market. It was the only maternity dress I ever had, because I never had money for new clothes, though fortunately I never got very big during my pregnancies.

One of the original quilts we'd had bought for Micah was a cute one with *Mr Men* pictures from the popular series over it. We called it the *Mr Men* blanket, and it somehow became Jim's favourite. If ever he had a headache or felt under the weather, he would lie on the settee and ask for it to go over him. It became a bit of a joke amongst us as he was very often lying on the settee under the *Mr Men* blanket. He was always complaining of being ill. Even our doctor got fed up with his constant trips to the surgery, and he generally refused to do a house call for him. The hospital knew him well too, as he'd had several exploratory operations to see what was wrong, and nothing was ever found.

One afternoon, Jim was under the *Mr Men* blanket and we were all watching television while little Micah played quietly on the floor with some toys. He was always such a good, contented, little boy, but suddenly he let out a huge howl that made us all jump.

"Whatever's the matter, Micah?" I asked, stooping down to him.

"I've got a toy toy up my nos!" he wailed.

So he did. It was a little yellow plastic peg from a hand-held solitaire game. We did all we could to try to get it out. When we blocked one nostril and told him to blow hard through the other one, he just sniffed it up even more! So that meant an embarrassing hospital trip, where the doctor removed it straight away with his tweezers, patted his arm, and said, "You won't do that again, will you?"

Jim took great delight in retelling the story at every opportunity, and when he got to the "toy toy up my nose" bit, he would always add, "It's a good job it wasn't a rocking horse!" We giggled the first time he said it, but after a time, it wore a bit thin.

What we did take from the incident was to not take anything for granted with our boy. We should have taken more notice of what he was playing with.

When I was getting quite near to my due date, Jim told me that the pub over the road was having a fancy dress evening the following Saturday and suggested we both should go.

He organised a babysitter and got out his trusty court jester outfit again, but unfortunately, I couldn't fit into my pixie outfit now so I had to think of something else. A couple of suggestions were thrown at me. For instance, Humpty Dumpty, but I wasn't sure how I could make that outfit. Another suggestion was a pregnant St Trinian's schoolgirl, but I thought that was rather bad taste. Instead, I went through my wardrobe for ideas. The best I could come up with, after sorting out from my cupboard a pretty, white, charity shop negligee, was a pregnant bride! I fixed a net curtain over my hair with clips and carried some plastic flowers in front of me.

It wasn't until much later, sometime after the event in fact, that I realised that was in just as bad taste as the pregnant schoolgirl. However, it was the best I could come up with at the time, and surprisingly, I won first prize! It was a giant, yellow, soft toy in the shape of a duckling. Not something I particularly wanted or needed, but it was so rare for me to have anything new for myself that I cuddled it for the rest of the evening in the pub, and when we got home, I put it on the floor next to me when we went to bed. I think I named it Ducky.

A few days later, Jim's brother came round to see us. He was living in nearby Thamesmead with his second wife and had come to tell us that she was expecting a baby now as well. On hearing this, Jim promptly gave him my Ducky for their new baby. I wasn't shocked, as he'd given my things away before without asking. I didn't actually need a giant duck teddy, but I was still hurt that my opinion as to whether to give it away didn't count for anything. It just went to remind me what a nothing person I really was.

CHAPTER 22

A Proper Council House

A FEW DAYS BEFORE MY baby was born, Jane Templer came round to see us with some good news. We were being offered a four-bedroom Council house in Crayford, the next town on. It had only taken us thirteen years since getting married to get a proper Council house! After all the temporary accommodation we'd had, it seemed like Jane had been with us all the way, encouraging us, and although her hands had been tied a lot of the time, she had seemed to be rooting for us all the way along. She'd become more like a friend than a housing officer, and that day we could've kissed her!

A couple of days after our good news, I was taken into hospital for bed rest as my blood pressure was very high. My baby wasn't due for several days, so I was told that once my blood pressure came down and stayed down for twenty-four hours, I could go home until I went into labour. But I remembered when I'd had high blood pressure in my previous pregnancy, I went home to rest and went into labour that same night, so I wasn't sure I would be coming home until the baby arrived.

That's exactly what happened too, that very same night. I felt the familiar pains and was trying not to groan too loudly from my hospital bed, but the other three girls in our section heard me and were calling to me, "Are you OK, Helen?"

Just then, a nurse bustled into the room and told us off for being so noisy in the middle of the night. I said that I thought I was in labour, but she didn't seem to believe me and just said, "Rubbish. Keep your noise down. You'll wake the rest of the ward!"

I staggered off to the toilet after she'd gone back to her desk, but in the few minutes I was in there, I had two more pains. I came out, leaned on the nurses' desk, and groaned, "I'm definitely in labour!"

She sent me back to my bed and said she'd be right there, and she quickly was. She had to help me back on my bed, then after pulling the curtains around me, she had a good feel of my stomach to see what was happening.

"Oh good gracious, Mrs Jones. You *are* in labour!" she squealed. Then she ran off, making more noise than we had fifteen minutes earlier!

A porter very quickly arrived and wheeled me off to the labour room, where I gave birth to another dear little boy within half hour of getting there.

The next day a surprised Jim and the children arrived. There was no way he could've got there for the actual birth.

I had a nice surprise that evening as well. A family from our Bible group came to visit me. I hadn't realised that anyone else had even heard that I'd had my baby, and as well as that, it was the weekend of a Bible convention. But my friends arrived afterwards, with their four children, all still in their Sunday best. I was so happy to see them.

I came home the next day with our new baby. He was blond with big blue eyes and beautiful, porcelain skin. His sister and brothers loved him immediately, and little Micah straight away stepped up to the mark as big brother. After some disagreements and discussion, we called him James.

The first afternoon home, baby James was lying in his baby bouncer when Micah was chatting away to him and decided to press down hard on the foot of the bouncer. Jim and I quickly grabbed the top of the bouncer! We both had visions of Micah letting it go and baby James flying through the front window! The children thought it was very funny, but my heart was pounding at what could have happened!

The next two weeks were spent getting ready for our move to Crayford. I had a chance to so show my new baby to my Erith friends and to say goodbye to them properly, although we weren't going far. As ever, the children thought it was yet another great adventure, even though it would mean a change of schools for them.

The day of the move soon came round, and Jim's brother Raif drove baby James and me to our new home, along with all the bits and pieces I would need for him. The other children went to their auntie's for the day, then Jim and Raif got on with the important business of helping the removal men.

Our new home was a semi-detached house with a big front and back garden. The day of the move was such a lovely, sunny day that I sat on my jacket in the back garden, nursing my baby and taking in the peace and tranquillity and general garden scents around me, along with the joy of finally having our own Council house.

I'd not been sitting there for long when I heard footsteps coming round the side of the house, and a voice calling out, "Hello! Anyone there?" Then there appeared a smiling lady a bit older than me with a cute, scruffy, black dog on a lead.

This was my first welcome from the Crayford Bible group, who'd obviously been told of our coming. This was Bessie and her dog, Tufty, who lived in the next road to ours, along with her husband and three teenage sons. She and her family became really good friends to us.

Another good friend I made in Crayford was Janet, who lived barely five minutes away. She belonged to the same Bible group and had children close in age to my older ones, and they all became good friends too. She also had a new baby called Chrissie who was almost the same age as my baby James, so they too grew to be good friends as time went on.

The Crayford Bible group actually met in Erith on Sunday mornings, so Janet and I would walk together with the children. It took us about three-quarters of an hour, but we were quite happy to walk with our pushchairs, with the older ones chatting and giggling away together. In fact, along with the meeting itself, the walk was the highlight of our week. That's because we could chat about anything and everything without our husbands taking over the conversation or interrupting us the whole time.

Janet and I would often visit each other for a ten-minute cuppa, but it never went well. Janet's husband was foreign, and for a start, I just couldn't understand his accent. I would nod and "hmm" at what I hoped were appropriate moments, and he would commandeer the conversation while my friend made the tea. Then when she brought the drinks in, she couldn't get a word in edgeways either.

It was pretty much the same when Janet came to me for a cuppa. Jim would never leave us in peace to chat either. He too would take over the conversation and would include a lot of joking and hurtful put-downs about me. Then when Janet had gone, he would very nastily refer to her as my lesbian friend, despite being as nice as pie to her face.

We did find a little way round this problem. There were four local shops on the estate, all within a ten-minute walk from my house. So if Janet needed one of the shops, she'd knock for me on her way and we'd walk round together and have a good natter.

Occasionally, Janet and I took our children down to Hall Place, where I'd spent some of my schooling. It was no longer used as a school and the gardens were open to the public, so we'd go there for a picnic as it was within walking distance for us. I'd made another good friend from the Crayford Bible group. This was Karen. She and Janet were already friends, and she would come on the bus to meet us there, as she lived a bit farther away. Karen had young children too, so we'd have a glorious afternoon with the children playing, running around, or paddling in the River Cray that ran through the gardens. The big ones would look after the little one, and we mums could chat as only mums can, and we laughed, sang, and made up silly poems to suit the occasion.

I did love Hall Place, and it felt good to be able to make some new memories there as opposed to my sad and lonely ones from my school days.

At the end of the afternoon, we'd wave goodbye to Karen and her children on the bus, and then Janet and I would troop wearily and happily back home, all going back to cook our husbands' dinners. I'd often get back and find Jim under the *Mr Men* blanket.

On a few occasions, Jim took us all down to Hall Place. It was a very popular place for families, and I was proud to show off my beautiful, old school annexe and gardens to him, almost as if they belonged to me. Unfortunately, even having the children with us didn't stop Jim from pulling me about there. He would just grab at me, and he was so crude and rough. There was nothing loving or romantic about it. If he hurt me, he'd tell the children I'd fallen over while they were busy playing.

More likely, he'd pulled or pushed me over. He didn't seem to care that it was broad daylight and others could see what he was doing, though immediately afterwards he'd have his arm "lovingly" around me. Why did he have to spoil everything? It was a special place to me.

I found a nice, little walk near our house. It was by the river, leading down to the shops in the town. It was only a twenty-minute walk along the road, and the river walk just put five minutes on top of that. The river ran behind the back gardens of the houses on that road. It took me longer still as I'd stroll along taking in the river atmosphere and the peace. If I had the children with me, we'd stop at one of the little bridges and play Poohsticks, where they'd excitedly watch to see whose stick came out the other side of the bridge first.

I made the mistake of showing Jim this little river walk to the shops one day when we went to town together. Unfortunately, it led to lots of late-night walks together when the children were in bed, with Melissa left in charge. I hated going when it was dark because there was hardly any lighting as it wasn't much more than an alleyway, and when he'd push me to the floor, I couldn't see if I was landing in stinging nettles or—worse—dog poo. He'd keep me there for what seemed like hours but was possibly only one, but it was more than long enough to be frightened and in distress. I tried to put up a fight because I really didn't want to have sex along a dark and dirty riverside path. I couldn't understand why he did either when we had a perfectly comfortable bedroom and double bed at home. But he always wanted more than sex in that alleyway. He always wanted me to wet myself. I loathed this, but who was I to have a say in anything? The longer I held off, the longer we were out.

One evening down this path, he decided he wanted me to do more than just wet myself. He wanted me to soil myself as well. I cannot bring myself to say much about this as I find it so absolutely disgusting. However, I did, out of fear, and he brought me home and bathed and changed me, murmuring lovingly as he did so. It made me feel physically sick. It happened several times over the years to come, but I shan't mention it again. It has left me with a massive repulsion to excrement of any kind now.

CHAPTER 23

Old Friends

THE CHILDREN SOON MADE FRIENDS with the other children in the street as there were a lot of little families on our side of the road. Melissa was one of the oldest of these, being 12 at the time we moved there, and they would all play together along the quiet street or in one of the gardens. Our house was on a slight bend, which meant our front garden was the biggest, so that was a favourite play area for them all—or the back garden, with our permission.

In our front garden was a huge, oak tree that the children loved to climb. One day a little boy from round the corner appeared and told the children they weren't allowed to climb the tree. Apparently, he and his family used to live in our house, and he claimed to have planted the tree, so it was his. A huge argument and fight ensued until the older children marched him back round the corner to his home. After a lot of discussion and calming down of the boy by his mum and big sister, the disagreement was finally sorted, and the little boy eventually became friends with them all. It turned out that the family *had* lived in our house before us, but of course, they certainly didn't plant the tree!

We'd stayed in touch with Raif's first wife, Brenda, and she would occasionally visit us with her five daughters. We hadn't seen them for some years, but they had moved to London so they'd come down on the train to visit us. The cousins were always happy to see each other, and sometimes we'd all go for long walks by the nearby River Cray, heading out towards the River Thames. It was too far to walk all the way, but it was a great walk beside all the wildlife, and the girls would often pick bunches of wildflowers along the way. Then we'd come back and have a lovely roast dinner, having left the meat to cook while we were out. It was always good to see them.

We hadn't been living in Crayford long when by chance we discovered that our old Sidcup neighbour Moira was living in nearby Erith with her son Danny. Roy was no longer on the scene, with them having parted company and him being in prison anyway. We hadn't seen them for a few years, and our boys were happy to see their old pal Danny again. We didn't see a lot of them, but we did visit her flat on a few occasions, and she drove over to us now and again for a cup of tea and a chat.

Another friend of Jim's from our Sidcup days was Brian, an old drinking pal, and we found that he was also living in Crayford with his wife and two children now. Brian was a big, Scottish giant of a man, and when we had known him back in Sidcup, his wife and children were still in Glasgow, but now he had brought them over to England, and he invited us all to meet his family and have dinner with them.

He and his family lived on the next estate to ours, and when we arrived at midday, his wife, Sandy, gave us each a plate of chips and some bread for our dinner. Unfortunately, I couldn't understand what Sandy said, so thick was her accent. I always seemed to have problems with accents! Their children, Doug and Cathy, were sent off to wash up afterwards, and then they and our eldest three children went off to play together. They were close in age to our older ones, Doug being maybe a little older, and they all seemed to hit it off straight away.

After our chips, Brian brought out the cider and poured us each a mugful. I wasn't much of a drinker so my mug lasted the entire afternoon, while the other three finished off several bottles as the afternoon wore on.

By the end of the afternoon, Brian and Sandy were completely drunk, and nothing they said was decipherable. Sandy kept dozing off in between her gabbling, and Jim was far from sober himself. Brian, however, had completely passed out on the floor. So Jim and I took our leave, calling for our children to come as well. But they were nowhere to be seen.

Jim said, "They're big enough. They know their way home. They'll come when they're ready."

Which was true enough. If our three went off to the field or the river, they always had strict instructions about coming home, and if anything happened to one of them, one was to stay with their sibling and the other to run home and get us. Melissa as eldest was always in charge and very sensible. Mark, the younger of the three, never knew what was what, where they were going, or where they'd been. He just followed them without question like a little lamb.

When we got back home, Jim got on the sofa with the *Mr Men* blanket, and I busied myself giving Micah and James their tea. I was just preparing to bath them both when I heard footsteps running round the side of the house, and all five children burst into my kitchen grinning and very grubby. Melissa and Cathy each had an armful of pretty, yellow gorse. I don't know how they'd picked it with their solid stems covered in thorns.

"We've been to Dartford Heath!" they declared.

I was very surprised as it was quite a way off and over some very busy roads. But I didn't have the heart to tell them off. I was just relieved they were back. From what I'd seen that day, I wondered if there'd be any tea for Doug and Cathy when they went home so I made beans on toast and eked it out between them all. Then I walked the two of them back to their estate and home. They protested at that. It seemed to me they were used to being independent. When we got there, Brian and Sandy were still asleep just as we'd left them a few hours earlier.

After just a few more drinking sessions with Jim, either at theirs or at ours, it became obvious that Brian and Sandy were both alcoholics. Despite that, Doug and Cathy certainly knew how to take care of themselves. They'd go knocking on doors offering to clean cars, and with the money they made, they would buy themselves something to eat, take it home, and cook it. Sometimes my three would help them. Another idea they had was to buy a book of raffle tickets then go from door to door selling them. Once they were sold, they would buy a little something for a prize—maybe a bottle of nail varnish or a bag of apples. They'd pick a random winner, then deliver the prize. Again, enough was left over to buy some food for themselves. I didn't interfere.

I couldn't afford to keep helping them myself, and I admired their innovation. Doug was probably only 13 at the time and Cathy a couple of years younger. I was very pleased to know that they had free school meals during term time.

One day Brian came over on his own for a drinking session with Jim. After a few hours, he staggered off to go home. We thought no more of it until through the evening there was a very loud knock on the door and there, with her hands on her hips, stood a very angry Sandy.

"Where is he then?" she demanded. "I know he's here. He only went out to get dinner." She marched in determinedly.

"He was here, Sandy, but he left hours ago," Jim protested.

After a suspicious look around, Sandy turned and went back out through the front door. As she stomped down the front path, with us looking out from the door, to our surprise, we all spotted Brian's huge frame lying prostrate between the front hedge and the rose bush. He was completely passed out, clutching a cider bottle to his chest!

A few weeks later, Brian arrived at our house carrying a battered suitcase, with Doug and Cathy trailing behind him.

"You weans go an play wiv ya pals!" Brian boomed at his children, and they ran off with my older three to play over the field. "I've left her," he told us. "I'm ganging back to Glasgee." He asked if he could have a bath at ours before he went to catch his coach.

Of course, we said yes. The front door was at the side of the house and was generally open in the summer for the children to come in and out. Our bathroom was next to the front door, so Brian left his opened case outside the bathroom door, taking out his clean vest and washbag, and went in for his bath.

Meanwhile, over the field and by the river were some men fishing, and they beckoned the children over to see a snake in the water.

A few minutes later, the five of them all arrived back here, breathless from running, with the snake in a bucket, but unfortunately, in their excitement, they dropped the bucket by the gate and the snake slithered away through the grass and couldn't be found.

Our next-door neighbour, an elderly man whose front door faced ours, came hurrying out at the commotion. He was very angry at the thought of a snake on the loose and was concerned that it could be a threat to the rabbits he kept in his back garden. Jim and I were just puzzled at the thought of a snake in the river. Somehow that didn't ring true to us. Anyway, the children ran off again to take the bucket back to the fishermen.

Shortly after that, Brian emerged from the bathroom, totally oblivious to the brief excitement a few minutes earlier, him being rather deaf as well as obviously preoccupied. He put his washbag back in the case, did it up as best as he could, and said goodbye to us. Then he headed off for his coach journey back to Scotland.

The children all returned after a while, and Doug and Cathy went back home to their mum, after sharing some cheese spread sandwiches I had made them all.

We thought no more about it until a couple of days later when we spotted a very interesting piece in one of the daily newspapers. It recounted how an African water snake was discovered in the luggage hold of a coach that arrived in Glasgow. It was apparently a complete mystery as to how it had got there, and it was captured and dispatched to a local zoo.

We did laugh at this as it solved our own mystery of the snake in the water. The snake, probably an abandoned pet, must have found its way into Brian's open case and curled up under his clothes. Then once on the coach, it must've slithered out of the split in the battered case. And as before, Brian most probably knew absolutely nothing about it!

After two or three weeks, we didn't see Sandy or the children anymore. We did wonder if they had gone back to Glasgow in the end as well, and I've often wondered what became of that enterprising young pair.

Around this time, Micah started at the local primary school, which was just a few minutes along our road, the older three all being at senior school by this time. It was an ordeal in itself just getting him there in the first place. Every morning he would claim that he couldn't walk and would lie on the floor along the path. We'd have to leave very early because he would crawl all the way on his hands and knees to school beside James in his pushchair, still claiming that he couldn't walk.

I came home after this daily ordeal one morning, ready to flop onto the settee with a cup of coffee, but to my horror, as I came through the front door, I could hear a familiar guffawing coming from the living room.

Another old friend had resurfaced.

Jonno was back.

CHAPTER 24

The Struggle Is Real

I HAVE NO IDEA HOW Jim and Jonno tracked each other down as we had moved a few times since our Sidcup days and Jonno had split from his wife and was living in a flat in Greenwich now.

Life was difficult enough without having Jonno back on the scene. Money was always tight, still. I rarely got any money from Jim, so I had to feed the family from the weekly family allowance payment, which was never enough to cover it all. Bessie round the corner often helped me out with little loans, which I always did my best to pay back. The Bible group leaders must have been aware of this as they gave Bessie a kitty that she could use when I needed help. I still paid it back as soon as I could, of course.

Another friend from our group who lived nearby was Linda. She worked in a bakery and at the end of the working week, the leftover cakes and bread were shared out amongst the staff. Later, at home, we would hear a knock on the door, and before we could open it, we would hear the *clip-clop* of high heels running down our front path. No one was there by the time we opened the door, but there on the step would be a bag of bread and cakes. We knew it was Linda, though she would never admit it!

I worked out how to make a very little go a long way. For instance, a vegetable soup mix, with added gravy and home-made dumplings, was a very cheap meal. Also, a small portion of minced beef with grated bread and potato added made it go twice as far. I found a good, little trick that helped me to put a meal on the table many a time. Around our estate were a lot of alleyways running between and behind the houses. If I took my time going through these alleys with my eyes glued to the ground, I could find pennies or other small coins lying in the dust and could often find enough to buy a pound of potatoes and a loaf of bread that would give us all a dinner.

My friend Janet and I both struggled financially, so we managed to get an evening cleaning job together. It was in a factory about ten minutes' walk away. It wasn't an easy job though. We had to use a huge, industrial machine each to polish the floors, and we both struggled with this, but we persevered for a few weeks. When I came home afterwards, I always had a huge sense of dread because it was through the evenings that Jim would insist on our "romantic" evening walks, while Melissa babysat. Not necessarily every evening, but two or three times a week. He would completely disregard the fact that I was tired after my job.

Often, as I came round the corner into our road after work, I would see Jonno's car parked by our house, and that would always churn my stomach. He would generally stay really late through the evening, drinking with Jim, and I would go to bed. But once Jonno had left, Jim would make me get up. He'd lay out what clothes he wanted me to wear, and we'd have to go over to the field by the river in the early hours of the morning. There were some public toilets in that field, and he just loved to push me into the men's ones, which were always smelly and filthy. Sometimes he'd want to have rough sex in there, and despite the time of night, I was still terrified that someone would come in. In fact, it did happen more than once as outlined in the first chapter. A couple of times when we came back, I saw that Jonno's car was still parked nearby. Was he spying on us? Jim told me I was imagining things, but I knew it was his car.

Sometimes in the field, he'd just push me over then jump on me and satisfy himself there. It could take a very long time though, probably due to all the drinking he'd done that evening. Or he would stand in front of me then suddenly grab my legs so I would fall heavily on my back. I tried to teach myself to fall without too much injury, but one time I hurt my neck badly and ended up at the hospital and had to wear a big neck brace for a while. I told people that I'd fallen over.

After a few weeks, Janet and I gave up the cleaning job. The work was just too heavy and exhausting, but we'd given it a good go.

From time to time, Jonno would give Jim some work painting and decorating with him again. I never saw any of the extra money, but it was nice not to have him home all through the day.

One afternoon while Jim was out working, my mother drove round to see us. She still lived in nearby Welling, but she didn't come often as she couldn't stand Jim, and the feeling was mutual, so that suited them both. I never used to tell her or my father anything about Jim's harsh treatment of me, but they did know I had money struggles and blamed him for that. On this occasion, my mother had brought a big bag of clothes from a jumble sale for my children and some sandals for me. She meant well, it was kind of her to go to jumble sales with us in mind, and she knew I could never afford new clothes for any of us. The younger boys wore whatever I put on them, but the older three definitely didn't like their nan's taste in suitable clothes for them. A knitted jumper with a picture of Noah's ark on the front did not appeal to my 12-year-old. The sandals for me were two or three sizes too big, but I said thank you just the same.

When their dad came home from work, the children laughingly showed him the jumpers that she had brought for them. I tried to tell them about being grateful and respectful, but they then grassed me up about the huge sandals that she'd brought for me.

"I like them," Jim stated. "Try them on."

I did tell him they were miles too big, but he insisted that I should put them on, so I did. I did the straps up as tightly as they would go, but there was still a good two inches to spare!

"Well, I really like them. Keep them and wear them just for me," he said, to my surprise. I wouldn't have liked them even if they had been in my size, but I tucked them under my dressing table with all my other shoes and hoped he would forget about them.

Fortunately, I never did have to wear those awful sandals; however, I did notice something strange a few weeks later on. I noticed that the straps had been loosened onto the largest fitting. It made me think and brought back a long-hidden memory from our early days together. Then I gradually started to notice a few other odd things. For instance, a couple of my elasticated skirts seemed to have become very loose, and one of my favourite dresses had the back zip broken, and it had been fine the last time I'd worn it. One of my blouses mysteriously had three or four buttons missing as well. I was incredibly upset at this.

Very often through the day, if Jim wasn't working, he'd disappear up to the bedroom for a couple of hours, without saying a word to me, which in itself was odd. Part of me wanted to go up and see what he was doing, as I had checked in the past and he seemed to be very keen on masturbating, which I thought was awful while I was around. But the thought of seeing him dressed in my clothes as well just repulsed me even more, so I couldn't bring myself to go and look. Now and again, afterwards, I'd discover an item of my clothing, which I knew I hadn't worn, in the laundry basket. I did once query this with Jim, and he claimed I must have left it lying on the floor and he'd spilled his cup of tea on it. I knew better than to argue with him. I had enough scars, both physical and mental, to last a lifetime without inviting any more.

Around this time, I had another shock. I was pregnant yet again. It seemed like any precaution we took was useless. We really didn't need another mouth to feed. I also worried about people judging us and calling us benefit scroungers as Jim was rarely working, just an odd week here and there with Jonno.

I gradually came to terms with the pregnancy. I didn't want the children to know I was unhappy about it. I never used to get very big when I was pregnant, so Jim and I thought it would be fun not to tell people and see how long it was before anyone noticed. I don't think we even told our children at first.

When I was around six months' pregnant, a hospital scan showed that I had placenta previa. This meant that the placenta was over my cervix, which was quite dangerous and could cause a miscarriage should the placenta come away. So for this reason, I had to go into hospital for complete bed rest until I had the baby.

I did feel a bit of a fraud in the hospital as I felt quite fit and well. I was told I wouldn't be allowed to go into labour naturally so would be booked in nearer the time for an early caesarean. In my naivety, I felt rather pleased about this. No ghastly labour pains for me this time. I'd just go to sleep after the anaesthetic then wake up with my new baby.

What could be better? OK, I'd feel numb at first, and it would be sore until the anaesthetic wore off. I was thinking of it along the lines of dental treatment! But wow! No labour pains!

I was put in the maternity ward in a section with four beds in. I was surprised to see one of Melissa's school friends in the bed opposite me, having her first baby. She could only have been 14 or 15. I was glad to see that she had a very supportive family visiting her.

It was so peaceful being away from Jim until visiting time. He'd been working with Jonno, so for the first three days I was there, he just came in the evening. He was a nightmare though. As soon as he arrived, he would pull the curtains around my bed and start mauling me intimately under the blanket. It was the very last thing I wanted at that time. At any time really, as I'd got to the point where I couldn't stand him touching me. But how could I stop him? Wives had very few rights in those days. I was no one whose opinion mattered. Just a nothing person.

While the other girls' husbands brought them flowers and chocolates and the like, all he ever brought in was a can of beer for himself. I couldn't wait for visiting time to be over.

On my fourth day there, I was moved into a side room by myself, and before it was even lunchtime, Jim turned up.

"You can't be here now," I said, panicking, "It's much too early for visiting."

That's when I discovered exactly why I was in my own little room. He had wormed his way around the staff on the ward to give him permission to come and go any time he pleased. He had claimed that it was very difficult for him on public transport as it was a long way, along with a sob story about the children because I was going to be away for a few weeks. I have no idea exactly what he said to them, but he was very clever with words and knew how to get his own way. I assumed that I was put in my own room so the other mums-to-be wouldn't get jealous. I wish I had known he was going to do that. I would have begged them not to allow it. But it was too late, and I never was very good at standing up for myself.

One or two of my friends from the Bible group discovered I was in the hospital and came to visit, but Jim was there the whole time and made it very uncomfortable for them. So instead of visiting, I would occasionally receive some nice "Thinking of you" cards from them.

I asked Jim what had happened to his work with Jonno, and he said he'd taken the time off to look after the children. When he actually looked after them, I have no idea as he was always up at the hospital. He loved it that I was in my own room now as it meant he didn't have to pull the curtains around anymore to start on his constant touching, stroking, and pawing me about.

One day Jim brought the children to the hospital with him. The two little ones had holes in their trousers, so I got them to climb up on the bed and then I stitched their trousers up for them. I was one of those mums who carried everything in her handbag, including needle and thread! I hugged them all so much. I'd really missed seeing them every day.

After two or three weeks there, I was told I could go home at weekends, so long as I rested completely. I was overjoyed at being able to spend the weekend with my children. There was something else I was looking forward to getting back to. I had been given a lovely organ. Jonno and Jim had been working in an old people's home and it was being thrown out so they had brought it home for me. I was thrilled! I'd always been able to knock a tune out on a piano so I soon adapted to this. I hadn't had it long before I went into hospital, so I was very eager to get back to it. A couple of the children enjoyed playing it after a fashion as well.

When the weekend arrived, Jim came with Jonno who gave us a lift back home. It was so good to be back with the children, although I did have to put up with Jim and Jonno drinking in my living room for the rest of the day while I sat there with my feet up as instructed. And of course, I had looked forward to a ten-minute play on my organ, but to my surprise, it was nowhere to be seen.

"Where's my organ?" I asked, suspiciously.

Then Jim explained that he'd lent it to a friend "because I didn't know you were coming home for the weekend, did I?" he replied, making it sound so matter of fact, as if lending an organ out for the weekend was a normal thing to do.

The following weekend when I came home, the organ was back in place, and I enjoyed a good little practice on it. And the same the weekend after.

So the routine went on. Five days in the hospital, and the weekend at home. I quite enjoyed the peace of being in hospital away from all Jim's nastiness, but of course, I still had to put up with him through the afternoons and evenings, mauling me about like a sex-mad schoolboy. I was sick of all this messing about.

When it got close to my due date, I was booked in for an elective caesarean section along with sterilisation. Much as I loved all of my children, I couldn't face the thought of having any more, and sterilisation was the only option left for us.

When the day arrived, I was very excited. Would I have a boy or a girl? I guessed another boy as I'd had five already. Jim was there with me, and I was given a general anaesthetic. I was so happy not to be having labour pains this time and couldn't wait to see and hold my new baby. Those thoughts flashed through my mind for just a few seconds, until I was completely out of it.

CHAPTER 25

The Joy of Having Teenagers

"WE'VE GOT A LITTLE GIRL, Helen," I could hear Jim saying as I came round from the anaesthetic.

"Are you joking?" I asked groggily. As if a dad would joke at a time like this!

Then it hit me. Pain. Real pain. Pain like I've never felt before. It was overwhelming, and I wanted to cry, until my little girl was gently laid on me and the happiness of that overtook the pain for those few moments.

It was so hard to take in the fact that I'd got another little girl, almost fifteen years after my first one, and it made everything worthwhile, even the pain. But I did feel rather cheated that no one had warned me just how painful a caesarean section would be! I guess everyone except for me thought it was obvious. At least I knew I wouldn't be going through it again, and I had ten days in the hospital still to get me back on my feet. Fortunately, I was quite quickly given some strong pain relief.

When I came home with baby Amanda, the children were thrilled to have me and their new little sister back. But where was the organ? Surely, he hadn't lent it out *again*, knowing I was coming home. Then Jim confessed the truth. He had actually swapped it for a stereo system. He'd just "borrowed" it back at weekends to postpone telling me the truth. I was so upset. We already had a stereo system. It wasn't the first time he'd either given away or sold my belongings, but it still hurt as it had been given to me. But my opinion never counted for anything.

By the time I came home with my new baby, most people had discovered from the children I'd been pregnant, but there were a few neighbours who were most surprised. After all, I'd barely had a bump when I went in.

I had to take it really easy for a while when I first got home, but I soon got back into the swing of things. It was still really difficult to make ends meet though. Jim had used the family allowance money each week while I'd been in hospital. I had felt obliged to give him the book as I couldn't use it there for anything. But when I asked him for it back, he refused. I tried looking for it with no success.

One day while Jim was out working with Jonno, there was a knock on the door. I was most surprised to see the greengrocer from round the corner standing there. I didn't know he and Jim were mates. But it wasn't a friendly visit. He was demanding twenty pounds that Jim owed for having goods on credit while I was in hospital. I felt so embarrassed and apologised on his behalf, promising I'd get him to come to the shop after work.

But as ever, Jim knew better than me and refused to go round to the greengrocer's shop. He just said, "I'll sort it when I get paid."

Then to add to the embarrassment, someone from one of the other local shops came knocking for money owed as well. I apologised again and said I'd get Jim to come round "as soon as he can" rather than saying after work that day.

This really upset me as we used these little local shops a lot and had always had a friendly relationship with the owners and the staff. I remember once going into the nearest shop with Jim and after we'd made our purchase, Mr Elliott, the owner, slapped a big bar of Cadbury's milk chocolate on the counter.

"That's for you, Mrs Jones," he declared.

"Why? What have I done to deserve this?" I queried.

"It's gratitude for how you've brought your boy up," he replied. Then he went on to tell us what had happened a few days before. Our Mark had gone to his shop to get something for us with a ten-pound note, and Mr Elliott had mistakenly given him change of twenty pounds. When Mark got home and realised, he ran straight back to the shop and gave back the extra money. "I don't know of any other young lad around here who'd be so honest," he said, beaming. "You must be so proud of him."

I was very proud of him, and without mentioning it, I knew that even Jim wouldn't have returned the ten pounds. He was always looking for a way to scam some money.

Apparently, every time Mark went into the shop after that, Mr Elliott would give him a little bag of sweets. In fact, they built up quite a rapport between them, and Mark used to say that he would like to work for Mr Elliott when he grew up.

But Mark didn't have such luck at the grocery shop round the corner. One day he came back from there very upset. He said that Mr Taylor, the shopkeeper, had told him off, but he didn't know why. "He said to me, 'Don't you ever do that again,'" Mark told us. "But when I asked him, 'What did I do?' he just said, 'You know what you did.' But I don't know."

Jim and I thought there must be some mistake here. Although Mark certainly wasn't perfect, he always had good manners when he was out and was always very honest. So we went round to the shop with him and asked Mr Taylor what the problem was.

He just said, "Your boy knows what he did."

"But he clearly doesn't." We told him. And then a thought struck us both at the same time. "You do realise that we've got two boys close in age, don't you?"

Well, it turned out that Mr Taylor had no idea there were two of them, and Scott, the older of the two, was always the naughty one, so we said no more but went home and brought Scott back with us.

Mr Taylor looked from one boy to the other, then back again, and he had to admit he'd always thought they were one and the same boy when they'd come into his shop! It turned out that Scott had pinched some sweets the day before, so we made him say sorry to Mr Taylor, who in turn apologised to Mark. He wasn't alone. A lot of people got the boys muddled up. And when they were growing up, I'd often been referred to as the lady with the twins, despite the fact that Scott was always a bit taller.

Poor Mark took a lot of stick from his older siblings. Being the youngest of the three, he used to go out and about with them, never having a clue as to where they were going. He just followed them like a little lost lamb. If there was a group of them, he was always the baby of the group.

Something that they always teased him about was Cyril. Now Cyril was a small teddy that Mark had been given as a small boy, and he took it everywhere with him. When he was tired or needed a bit of comfort, he would hold Cyril with three fingers and thumb, and the other finger would go in his mouth. Quite cute as a very small child, but unfortunately, he just couldn't give up this habit. Scott and Melissa did manage to stop him from sucking his finger in public but couldn't get him to part with Cyril. So poor Cyril was always in the wars too. They put him in the dustbin several times, but Mark found him and fished him out. He got hidden in the oven, in a neighbour's car's exhaust pipe, and even in the toilet system a few times. They once made a string noose and hanged Cyril from the tree in the front garden. I was always having to wash the poor teddy to placate Mark. One day they cut Cyril's head right off! Would that put an end to it? No. Because this softy of a mother stitched it carefully back on again. I don't remember how old Mark was when he finally broke the habit, but he was definitely in double figures!

One afternoon, Scott and Melissa almost came to blows in the back garden. It started off as a water fight together, then Scott thought he would go one better. He ran into the bathroom, grabbed a perfume bottle, and then ran back out and sprayed it at his sister. He got Melissa in the eye and she screamed loudly, at which her dad ran into the garden and straight away gave Scott a huge clout round the head, knocking him to the floor. Next thing, Scott was down there crying and with blood streaming from his nose. I could see it was a hospital job for them both, so I ran round to my friend Bessie in the next road, and she sent one of her sons back with me to take them in his car. Jim went with them, Melissa holding her eye and Scott holding his nose. I stayed home with the little ones.

They told a funny story when they got back. Apparently, Melissa was seen first to have her eye washed out, and the doctor asked her, "How did this happen?" When she said her brother had done it, he replied, "Where is he? I'll punch him on the nose!"

"No need to," she replied quickly. "My dad's already done it, and he's next."

It turned out that Scott had a broken nose, thanks to his dad. I felt so sad about that because Scott hadn't done it to hurt her. He just hadn't realised the danger. His dad had such a quick temper and was very handy with his fists. It was usually towards me, but Scott often copped it as well. But I have to say that when Scott reached his teens, he did become very difficult. He had always been stubborn, and unfortunately, he and his dad never got on.

I remember another time when his dad got mad at him, though I forget the reason why. But he gave Scott a huge push, and he fell to the floor, his knees landing in the cat's plate of dinner, sending food flying and smashing the plate. He was only wearing shorts that day so I got him to sit on the worktop, and took a long time picking the tiny bits of china out of his knees. Jim's brother was visiting at the time, and before I had finished, he came charging in the kitchen and gave Scott a big shove, smacking his head against the wall cupboard behind him and telling him he should have more respect for his father. So now he had a bleeding head as well. I mopped him up and cleaned the cat food and the rest of the china pieces from his knees as best as I could. Later on, I shut myself in the bathroom and cried.

Things went from bad to worse between Jim and Scott, and social services were involved. We all went to family therapy where each of us played "happy families", leaving them none the wiser about our problem boy. He was then assigned a social worker who tried to talk to him. I've no idea whether Scott told his social worker about the real sorry situation at home, but he got taken out by him a lot to McDonald's, bowling, and various other activities. All things we could never afford to do with our children.

One day Mark asked, "If I start being naughty, will I get to go to McDonald's?" It was heartbreaking. How could we answer that?

It got to the point where Scott was heading for foster care. Of course, I didn't want to lose him, but on the other hand, it would mean he was away from his dad. In the end, our friend Moira offered to have him live with her and Danny as a temporary foster carer, so this was arranged. It meant he didn't have to change schools and he was near enough to keep contact, so we still saw him sometimes.

Melissa was always a huge help to me with the little ones. She was a natural little mother, helping to bath and dress them and more. When she got to her mid-teens, Jim would never let us be on our own together.

If she came into the kitchen for a mother-daughter chat while I was busy there, he would come in and send her back to the living room or he'd just make a point of staying in the kitchen as well. It seemed as if he resented our natural relationship. Sometimes he would mutter something about lesbians, but I couldn't I believe he'd really think that about us. He used to accuse me and my friend, Janet of this as well. He had always been very homophobic, to the point of swearing profusely if anything was ever mentioned on the television about the gay community.

When I was first out of hospital with Amanda, I asked Melissa how things had been while I was away. At first, she said it was all OK and that she had spent a lot of time looking after her two youngest brothers. I'd guessed at that because we had been having a lot of trouble getting her to school for a while. I knew Jim would have taken advantage of that situation.

Eventually, Melissa did tell me more about how things had been while I was in hospital, and it made me feel very sad. She told me how her dad would give her some money to go and buy some dinner for them all, and she'd think, *I can get something really good with all this.* And before she'd got out of the door, he'd call her back and tell her to get him some beers and cigarettes out of the money, and that would take half of it at least. She said this happened every time.

She told me about another evening when her friend Nikki knocked on the door. She asked Melissa, "Is your dad in?" Melissa said yes, and Nikki beckoned her outside to tell her something in private. She had been to a family party earlier that day and there was a lot of finger food left over so Nikki had bagged some of it up and brought it round, and tucked it under the hedge in the front garden.

Later that night, when everyone including her dad was asleep in bed, Melissa crept downstairs and out of the door to retrieve the goody bag. Then back inside, she woke her brothers up, took them all into her bedroom, and there they shared a delicious midnight feast thanks to Nikki's kindness. Whenever I try to picture this, it brings tears to my eyes.

We did try to get Melissa back in school. She only had another compulsory year to do. We had the truancy officer round more than once, to no avail. One afternoon her form teacher paid us a visit to try to persuade her back. He sat on the settee next to her, talking so nicely that we started to warm to him. We joined in the discussion, trying to convince her to go back to school. Just when we all thought we were getting through to her at last, he said, "OK, Melissa, we'll see you on Monday then," and he started patting and stroking her knee, rather too eagerly.

Once he'd gone, we both said, "You're not going back now, Melissa." And she didn't.

CHAPTER 26

New Neighbours

WHEN AMANDA WAS STILL TINY, I got a home typing job to help the dire financial situation we were always in. I'd been begging Jim to give me back the family allowance book but to no avail. A couple of weeks later, Jim drove up to the house in a second-hand blue Ford Cortina.

"This is mine now!" he said proudly, jangling a set of car keys, and the children all ran out excitedly to have a look.

"How on earth did you afford that?" I questioned. "And we won't all fit in it, will we?"

"It's mine. It's paid for. Come on, kids. I'll take you for a drive." And the five children all jumped in and he sped off, leaving me there with the baby.

I always relished a bit of peace, but I couldn't help but worry about how he could afford to buy a car, albeit a second-hand one.

I found out a week or so later. He'd bought the car from neighbours round the corner. I didn't know them well, but I passed the wife in the street one day and she asked me, "How's the car?"

I had no idea it had come from them. I just said, "It's fine." And I couldn't stop myself from adding, "I don't know how Jim got the money for it."

That's when she explained. Jim had signed the weekly family allowance book over to her and her husband so they could cash it each week until the car was paid for. I was shocked. I said I wanted my book back, but she refused, saying they had made a deal. And as Jim's name was on the book as well as mine, he was entitled to do that.

I was devastated. I thought that it was illegal to sign your book over like that and thought of reporting it to the authorities. But then, my name was on the book too so I thought that would put me in trouble as well. I went round to see her again a few days later and said if she gave me the book back, I would get Jim to pay the money himself or return the car even. (Not sure how I would have managed that.)

But she still refused. "A deal's a deal," she said.

So that's when I got the home typing job. My friend Janet was working and I looked after Chrissie for a couple of days a week as well. James loved having his little playmate round, and they played happily while I typed away and baby Amanda slept in her carrycot.

The car didn't last long. After just a few weeks, it was gone. Jim said the car was no good. Not worth anything and dangerous to drive. I questioned him about getting his money back and the family allowance book, but he wouldn't discuss it with me. I'm guessing he really sold the car on, but I never got to the bottom of what actually happened to it.

After several more weeks, we did, at last, get our family allowance book back.

One afternoon I was typing away; it was either a Saturday or after school because the older children were home and having a lot of fun. I could hear them banging about and laughing. They had got their quilts off their beds and were sliding down the stairs on them. Being a soft touch, I let them get on with it. They were happy.

All of a sudden, I heard a huge crash and went running to see what had happened. Their friend Ian, a wiry little lad from up the road, had thought he would go one better without a quilt, so he curled himself up into a ball and rolled down the stairs and straight through the window at the bottom! Lucky Ian, he didn't have a scratch on him.

Although life was stressful, there was always a lot of fun with the children. Mine all got on well, apart from the occasional teasing and play fighting. One Saturday when Brenda visited with her girls, the children all played at competing at the Olympics, along with children from the street, so there was a big crowd of them. They organised races of all sorts—skipping, jumping, and running races round the block.

Even I joined in. Some of the children cheated and cut through the back alleys, so they came first. Nobody minded. It was just for fun, and there were no prizes. I think I'd made some buns so everyone got one of those at the end.

The elderly couple next door moved away and a very young couple with a little girl and a new baby moved in. This was Brad and Sam. Whenever our front doors were open at the same time, their little girl would always run in to see us, our doors being opposite each other at the side of the houses with no dividing fence. She was a dear, little girl, and she sometimes came and helped me bake cakes and would take some home for her mum and dad. Her mum worked full-time and her dad was a househusband. He taught my younger boys to ride bikes. I was happy with that because Jim never had much time for the children.

As their little boy got bigger and learned to walk, he would dart into our house like a rocket and leap on the furniture! I'd never seen a boy like it. He was a real live wire. One day Brad was in our house, sitting on the settee with Jim and watching football on the television. His little boy darted through our front door, into our living room, and quickly climbed up the back of the settee and did a roly-poly over it, landing neatly between Jim and his dad. Brad had no idea his little boy could even do that!

Brad became quite a good friend to us both. Sam was lovely too, but we didn't see so much of her due to her work commitments. The children would come and go between the two houses and gardens as they pleased throughout the summer.

Brad became quite a hit when his little girl started school, being the only male amongst all the mums. He didn't seem bothered by it. When he came home from dropping her off and I came back from taking my little boys, he nearly always made me a cup of milky coffee, just how I liked it, and would call me over the back fence to have a coffee and a chat together. He was quite a sweetie, though a lot younger than me. I did have a cheeky thought though, which I never voiced, but what would all those flirty mothers think if they knew?

I never asked him. I just couldn't. But I did wonder if he was nice to me because he'd overheard or even seen Jim's harsh treatment of me. I felt sure that he must have, although he never let on if he had.

Jim's "romantic" walks with me continued. Melissa would babysit and we would go off down by the river. If he had any money, we would start off in the Jolly Farmers, our local pub. He would never let me use the toilets there and I knew exactly why, but I do remember once when he went off to the gents', I hurried off to the ladies' as soon as he'd gone. Unfortunately, he was out before me, and he was furious. He bought another beer for himself and a cider for me to try to refill my bladder. Then off we went for our river walk.

There would usually be a few dog walkers along the way, and I was always afraid they would see my humiliation as I lay on the grass or recognise me even. I did sometimes ask Jim if we could just have a nice walk and save the lovemaking for back home in bed. He'd say yes but would always go back on his word. I couldn't understand it when we had our perfectly comfortable bed back at home.

It wouldn't be long before he would start kissing me, then pushing or pulling me over. I really couldn't think of it as "lovemaking" though. There was nothing loving about it. Usually, I would be really cold as well because the clothes he would lay out for me to wear before we left home were usually skimpy, mismatched clothes and shoes unsuitable for the rough walk by the river. It would be a huge relief when we headed back home, but even then, he would often still be stopping for ages to pull me about or even take my clothes off. He was especially fond of getting my clothes off by our house, and then there would be more humiliation in the back garden. That's why I wondered if Brad had seen this from his bedroom window—or any other neighbour.

By the time we actually came indoors, it would be the early hours of the morning and my legs would be really sore from having been wet and cold as well as being sore in other places from the rough treatment I'd had. There just seemed to be no respite from it.

But I did get a little respite. I had to go into hospital for a full hysterectomy and was going to be in for ten days. I hoped and prayed that Jim wouldn't get round the nurses this time to allow him unrestricted visits. Fortunately, he didn't, as ten days was nowhere near as long as the last time I was in, and it soon went by.

Jim picked me up in his brother's car to bring me home, and I went straight upstairs to bed as I felt so rough still. I was told to take it easy for six weeks.

The second evening that I was home, Brad next door was having a bonfire, along with baked potatoes and toasted marshmallows, and he invited us to join them. I said to the children, "Enjoy yourselves."

"You're coming too, Mum," they replied. "Brad's put an armchair in the garden for you to sit on."

And he had. He'd even put an upturned bucket there for my feet to go on, and he made me a milky coffee while he and Jim both had a beer. I was touched by his thoughtfulness and it was an enjoyable evening. Brad was a good neighbour.

CHAPTER 27

A Moment of Realisation

THE TYPING WORK HAD ALREADY come to an end, so when I recovered from my surgery, Janet and I each got a job in the Sunshine Cafe in town. My Scott worked there on a Saturday, washing down the backyard. When he left, Mark did the job, and later on, Micah did it when he was only about 10 and earned a fiver for it. A lot of money then for a young lad.

Janet and I enjoyed working together. We got to know a lot of the customers as Crayford was just a small town and they were mostly regulars coming in. I remember one regular who had the biggest and bushiest moustache and beard that I'd ever seen. He always ordered a cup of tea and a straw to drink it with. He never ordered anything to eat, and I couldn't help but wonder how he managed at mealtimes.

There was a girl with multicoloured hair and fancy clothes who came in quite often. We looked forward to her coming as she was like a ray of sunshine. Quite a change from the usual overall-clad workmen who frequented the cafe.

The perks of working there were a free lunch every day that we worked and pudding as well. The blackberry crumble with ice cream was a huge favourite with us both. The cook made it fresh every day. Jim cooked the evening meal when I got home from work, so that was an added bonus.

The two of us worked there together for some time until changes were made that made it difficult for us, and sadly we both left. We had enjoyed our time there and have lots of fond memories.

I still needed to work to make ends meet. It made no difference whether Jim was working or not. I rarely got any money from him. By this time, Melissa was working for a local agency and had been going regularly to a fruit packing factory, so I registered with the agency and got a couple of weeks at the same place.

It was fascinating. I'd never worked in a factory before. I loved watching the boxes going along on a conveyor belt above our heads and oranges coming along on a waist-high track. There was other fruit going along elsewhere in the factory. I could have watched it all for ages, but of course, I had a job to do. We had to pull out any odd oranges that came along the track, and I did this alongside my daughter.

Around this time, Jim started working for someone who lived nearby, and he had the use of the work van. The job lasted for a few months, but financially it didn't help me at all. I just managed with the money that I had earned at the fruit factory and Melissa's contribution towards her keep.

One day Jim came home from work and said it was his boss's birthday and we'd been invited to a local club to celebrate at the weekend. Jim's brother Raif was going as well. He had been lodging with us for a while as he'd split from his second wife.

All my memories of going to parties with Jim were bad ones, and I tried my hardest to get out of going. I didn't even know his boss. But again, I didn't have any say in it and found myself forced into going. I hoped that with his brother going as well it, would be OK.

Saturday came, Melissa babysat, and the three of us went off to the club. I wanted to stay alert so I only drank orange juice. I wasn't much of a drinker anyway. I felt rather like the proverbial fish out of water as I mostly sat at the table by myself while Jim and Raif joked around with his boss and workmates. I hated the crude way they talked and joked, and I'm sure they all thought I was a prude.

After we had been there some time, Jim told me we were going on to a proper party with the boss after the club had closed. I dreaded this and tried saying I would be too tired, but Jim promised I could have a long lie in the next morning and he would get up with the children.

Then he and Raif tried to persuade me to have a "proper" drink, and I refused. But Raif kept asking what my favourite drink was, and in the end, I agreed to a small glass of Bailey's. It was a drink I loved but rarely had, so it was a treat, and I thought I would make it last as long as possible. Jim went to the bar to order my drink so I slipped off to the ladies' while his back was turned. When I came out of the toilets, there, tottering along in a pair of extremely high heels, was a very overly made-up man in drag. I had never seen anyone like it before, except on television. He must have seen my surprise as he gave me a huge, exaggerated wink and said in a deep voice, "Allo, dahling!"

I couldn't get back into the hall quick enough.

As I approached our table, I saw Jim sprinkling some white powder into the Bailey's he'd just bought me, and he started to shake the glass, stopping abruptly when he saw me coming. Then he left the table.

I asked Raif, "What's in my drink?"

"It's nothing," he replied. "Don't worry about it."

Clearly it wasn't "nothing", so I wouldn't drink it and poured it into someone's half-empty, abandoned glass. I guessed it was some sort of drug, and I was determined not to be tricked into taking anything. When Jim returned to the table, he claimed not to know what I was talking about when I questioned him.

Then the drag queen appeared. The act wasn't really to my taste, but what did he do? He made a beeline for me as we'd already met and teased me mercilessly throughout his act. I was so embarrassed but couldn't help giggling to try to cover it up.

As the evening drew to an end, I started to dread the thought of going on to a party. Outside in the club car park, Jim, Raif, and his boss seemed to be in deep discussion for ages, while I stood there getting cold. Eventually, I managed to get Jim's attention to unlock the van so I could wait inside. When they came back to the van, I was very relieved when they said we were just going home after all.

Early one evening, after Raif had moved out, Jim said he would take us all out in the van. When I asked where we were going, he said he didn't know yet. Just an evening drive. We set off heading towards London, and after a while, he pulled up outside some shops in Greenwich. It turned out to be Jonno's place. He appeared, let us in, and led us upstairs to his little flat above a hardware shop.

He made me a cup of coffee and gave the children some squash, and he and Jim sat drinking cans of beer. The television was on, but we couldn't really watch it over the pair of them chatting and laughing. It was all rather boring, and after a couple of hours, I was pleased when Jim said we ought to be heading back home. I think he'd noticed that the younger children were falling asleep.

So we all trooped back down the stairs, Melissa carrying Amanda, and got into the van. But Jim and Jonno seemed to be talking for a long time behind the van, so I got back out and peered round the corner at them.

They were kissing!

I got back in the van quickly, hoping they hadn't noticed me. I was shocked! Or was I? I had a sudden realisation of what was what, and all sorts of things from over the years finally slipped into place. Things that at that moment I couldn't have put into words or made sense of.

The thought struck me as Jim got back into the driver's seat. *How could a husband prefer another man to his wife?* It just seemed to remind me of how insignificant I was. A nothing person really.

CHAPTER 28

Loss and New Life

ONE MORNING THERE WAS A knock on the door. It was my mother and Hannah, and they were both crying. My father, who had never had good health, had died in the night. Our mother had phoned Hannah straight away and she had driven down from Berkshire. Then they had driven over to tell me. We all stood in the kitchen with our arms around each other, crying. He had been such a mild-mannered and likeable man. In fact, well-loved by all who knew him. Jim looked after the children, and I went back to my mother's with them.

I wanted to have one last look at my dad who was upstairs laid out in bed, but our mother said not to because the doctor had been and "messed him about", as she put it, so he didn't look nice or natural now. I felt upset at this but couldn't go against my mother.

When I went upstairs to use the bathroom, I was tempted to creep along the landing and peep in at him, but when it came to it, I didn't dare. I really didn't want to upset my mother. She was distraught enough as it was.

A big crowd attended his funeral at the crematorium. Jim and the children came with me. It was such a sad and difficult day. Some of my mother's friends had kindly opened their home for refreshments afterwards and she took my three eldest children with her. Jim was not welcome because of my mother's feelings towards him, and because most of the guests were from the Bible group and he was still not in good standing with the group. I suppose people thought I was being loyal to my husband by going off with him, but really, it was out of fear.

I so wanted to spend some time that day with people who had loved my dad.

Jim and I took our younger children to a cafe in Blackfen for a drink before heading home on the bus. Later that day, my mother and Hannah brought the older ones back.

A year or so after my father's death, Mark was having some problems at school, so Jim and I managed to get him transferred to the Welling school that was opposite my mother's house. He went on the bus and occasionally would pop in to see his nan in his lunch hour and have his packed lunch there. I'm sure she really enjoyed his visits being on her own now, and I think too that she recognised his good heart as she was very fond of him, despite her love of telling grandchildren off!

More than once on a Saturday, when I was struggling to manage, Mark would go out and find the milkman, help him on his round for the morning, then come home and give me the bit of money he had earned. He wasn't a regular helper, but he was so likeable and conscientious that the milkman was always happy to have his help.

One Saturday was a convention day for the Bible group, and we were all meeting together at Crystal Palace. It was easily accessible from Crayford by bus, but unfortunately, I didn't have the fare as I wasn't working at that time. I had asked Jim, and he said he would give me the bus fare in the morning, so the evening before, I got a packed lunch prepared for the children and me and got our best clothes ironed and laid out ready for the morning. But when the morning came, Jim didn't have any money for us after all. I was so disappointed. But again, Mark said to me, "I'll get you the bus fare, Mum." And off he went to find the milkman.

He came back late morning and gave me his earnings and tips, and I set off with the three little ones on the bus. We had our packed lunch in the park, then went into the venue for the afternoon sessions. We met up with some friends there who gave us a lift back home afterwards. We'd had a really good day, thanks to Mark's kindness.

By this time, Melissa had had a couple of different boyfriends, and now she was seeing a local lad named Tom. We all liked him, and because he was always at our home, little Amanda thought he was another brother and treated him as such. In fact, we all accepted him and treated him as family.

One afternoon Tom had come round to see Melissa, who was in the bathroom doing her hair and make-up, so he was waiting at the side of the house where there were a lot of youngsters chatting and playing between the two houses. Brad and Sam were sitting on their doorstep watching their little ones, and I was in my garden pegging my washing out.

Suddenly, I heard a loud smash and Melissa screaming. I dashed into the bathroom to see what was wrong. She was standing in the empty bathtub, shaking and with blood on her face. "What's happened?" I asked, but she was clearly in shock and couldn't speak.

"Out here, Helen!" someone shouted.

I rushed out of the front door to see Scott sitting by Sam on their doorstep with a bloodied tea towel wrapped around his hand and blood all over the floor.

Apparently, he had put his arm out to lean on the wall by the bathroom and had completely misjudged it. His hand had gone full force through the window and into his sister's face as she stood there brushing her hair in the mirror. No wonder she was in shock!

Melissa soon calmed down, she washed Scott's blood off her face, and she and Tom took Scott to the hospital. Jim and I followed shortly afterwards. It was a really bad injury. He'd sliced through the tendons in his hand and we were told that after the needed surgery, it could limit the use of his hand. He had the surgery and was kept in overnight. Fortunately, once it had healed, Scott had no problem with it.

I was still struggling with my feelings for Jim. I had got to the point where I just couldn't stand him touching me anymore. He had killed any feelings that I'd ever had for him, as I definitely had cared about him, and up to a point I still did, but he had hurt me so much, physically, emotionally, and sexually. I put on a show of being happy though. I didn't want Tom to realise what a fractured family we really were. Melissa also struggled with her relationship with her dad, and I wanted to see her happy with someone and hoped that someone would be Tom.

Jim still insisted on our evening walks, and Tom and Melissa would both babysit for us. We used to be out for hours at a time while my nightmare treatment took place, generally by the river. I would be tripped over, pushed into the public toilets, have clothes ripped off, and have rough, painful sex, front and rear. I would sometimes be in agony when we got home.

One evening Jonno had been round drinking with Jim, then when he left, Jim took me out for our walk. But that time, he was hurting me so much that I did the only thing I could think of to make him stop. I kicked him as hard as I could in his privates. He staggered back briefly then lunged at me again, full of fury. He didn't even cry out, which surprised me because at home, if one of the little ones jumped on his lap, he would scream out in agony!

When we finally came home, I noticed that Jonno's car was parked at the bottom of our road and mentioned it to Jim. But he said it wasn't his. Once indoors, he pushed me into the bathroom and stripped me off. Then after washing my wet legs, he started kissing and fondling me. Suddenly I noticed a flicker of light from the wall adjacent to the kitchen. I knew a big piece of plaster was missing from the bathroom wall there and realised it must go right through to the kitchen, where it was hidden by some hanging aprons and tea towels. I shouted to Jim, "Someone's spying on us from the kitchen!"

"Don't talk such rubbish," he snarled.

I managed to grab a towel around me and run out of the front door, just in time to see Jonno's car drive off. Jim said I was imagining things. But I knew what I'd seen. How often had this happened? That hole had been there a long time, and Jim seemed to enjoy messing about with me in the bathroom. Now I knew why.

I discovered a hole in the bathroom ceiling as well, but to look through that one, you'd have to lift the rug up in the bedroom. I felt sure that Jonno must have been upstairs several times spying as well, though I couldn't prove this. I was also worried for my Melissa. Had anyone spied on her while she was in the bath?

The bathroom incident definitely had happened several times. I was sure of this and was always poking bits into the hole to try to block it. I couldn't bear this situation anymore. I wished that Jim would just leave. His brother had left two wives and several girlfriends. *Why couldn't Jim do the same?*

One day, one of our Bible group leaders said that two of them would like to see me, and they would pick me up one evening to take me to one of their houses to have chat. I was really worried about this. Had I done something wrong? My thoughts went back to the 13-year-old me who was in trouble over the ring. Had I been spotted on one of our awful night-time ordeals?

I saw Bessie the next day and told her how worried I was about it. She must have phoned one of them up and told them because she popped round later and assured me they just wanted to see if I was OK and if I needed any help in any way.

When I did see them, they were so kind. They asked me how things were at home, and for a brief moment, I considered telling them. But I just couldn't find the words or the strength to, even though they had said, "Remember, we can't help you if you don't tell us what is wrong." They asked if I was managing financially, and I said I was, although it was a struggle. They said to let them know if I needed anything for the children, such as school clothes. But I didn't feel that we did at that time. Along with Janet, I was a good customer of our local charity shop and had even got a blazer with the correct badge on it when one of my boys started senior school.

When they drove me home afterwards, I felt so relieved and happy that someone was listening to me, but as soon as I got home, the familiar feeling of dread returned, giving me an actual pain low down in my stomach. I never knew what mood Jim would be in when I came home from anywhere, and this time as soon as I got through the door, he straight away asked me, "Have you been talking about me?"

"No, of course not," I replied truthfully, and I told him how kind they had been.

He suggested I should have told them that we all needed new shoes to try to get some money out of them. Typical Jim.

Our son Mark was still going to the Welling school opposite my mother's house, but since my father had died, she had really struggled with being on her own. In the end, she put the house up for sale and arranged for an annexe to be built on Hannah's house, ready to move in with her and her husband in their Berkshire home.

I thought a lot about my years growing up in that house and wrote a poem of good memories to give my mother when she moved out. I had written loads of little verses and poems for her over the years, usually funny little ditties to make her laugh. I'd been doing that since I was a child. She actually said to me, not long before leaving her Welling home, "You'll have to write a poem."

I told her, "I already have. You'll get it when you move."

She was expecting a few humorous verses, but she got a long, sentimental poem with all my best childhood memories.

The evening before her move, I copied the poem out neatly for her and popped it in a card that I gave to Mark to give his nan before school. He didn't stay to see her reaction, but she told me later that it had made her cry! Not the reaction I had expected.

Meanwhile, Tom and Melissa's relationship seemed stronger than ever. They seemed so happy, and I was happy for them too.

They were celebrating something, possibly their six-month anniversary. I knew that neither of them had any money, so for a surprise, I made them a Victoria sponge. When it had cooled, I cut it very carefully into a heart shape, iced it, and piped buttercream flowers on top. It took me a very long time to get it looking as nice as I could, then I hid it in the cupboard from Melissa.

When Tom arrived at our house, I quietly beckoned him into the kitchen to show him the cake. The idea was that he would bring it into the living room and present it to Melissa as if it was from him. But I didn't want to say anything out loud, so I tried to tell him this by signs and waving my arms about! Thinking he'd got the gist of it all, I went and joined Melissa and the rest of the family in the living room.

A couple of minutes later, Tom came in, but not with the cake.

"Wasn't there something in the kitchen Tom?" I asked, cryptically.

"Yes. It was lovely. Thank you."

I dashed back to the kitchen to discover that he had totally misunderstood all my arm-waving and cut a huge chunk out and eaten it!

Melissa had made friends with Mandy, a young mum who lived a few doors down from Bessie in the next road. Sometimes she babysat her three boys. They were lively little boys, always in trouble and never without cuts and scrapes on their knees. But Melissa, ever the little mum, always had them under control.

One day, Melissa told me that Mandy had asked to see me, so we walked round there together. Mandy made us both a cup of tea, then she said, "Melissa's got something to tell you."

I looked from her to my daughter and guessed what she was going to say.

"I'm pregnant, Mum," she muttered, looking at the ground.

"I know," I replied. I didn't really, although there had been one or two little signs that now added up. Then she started to cry. "Have you been to the doctor?" I asked gently. But she hadn't. So the next day, we went down to the doctor together, where it was confirmed. Still no home pregnancy kits in those days.

Our doctor was a lovely Indian lady. She knew of my religious leanings and looked at me worriedly. Then she asked how I felt about it as her mother.

"Well, I'd be happier if she and Tom were married, but she's my daughter and I love her, so if she needs me during her pregnancy, I'm here."

Our doctor was visibly relieved to hear that. Being a large family, she knew us well, especially Jim, as he was always there claiming to be ill. In the end, she refused to see him anymore, so he had to transfer to a different doctor's surgery on the other side of town. He insisted that we all changed to the new doctor, which I was really sad about. However, that was a year or so later on.

Once we'd all come to terms with a new baby coming, the family was excited. We got to know Tom's family, who were very nice, respectable people. We warmed to them as well as to Tom.

As Melissa drew nearer to her due date, Tom managed to rent a room for them just a short walk away from us. They seemed happy with it, although we still saw quite a lot of them.

When her baby arrived, there was great excitement all round. She had a beautiful, little girl and they called her Eliza. Amanda was only 2 years old, and we joked that Melissa had waited so long to get a sister that she had her own! Tom, his family, Jim, the children, and I all went to the Jolly Farmers to celebrate. The children had a great time on the swings and slide in the pub garden, and Tom's mum and I both proudly sported a pink "I'm a grandma" brooch. I wasn't sure if I felt like a grandma. I wasn't even 40!

The next day, when Melissa was home with her baby, we went round to see her. Their room was just inside the front door and it was dominated by the huge double bed. I wondered how they managed in one room, although they did have use of the kitchen and bathroom. But Melissa looked well and happy cradling her new daughter, and that was the most important thing.

So now there was a brand-new life in the family.

CHAPTER 29

From Bad to Worse

IT WAS A REAL JOY to watch Eliza thrive. She was a gorgeous, chubby, little girl with dark, curly hair like her dad, and we all loved her unconditionally. They spent a lot of time at our house, and we saw Eliza taking her first steps and saying her first words. She and Amanda were best friends with only two years between them. More like sisters than auntie and niece. I even managed to get the two of them matching outfits from our local charity shop.

We still saw a lot of Scott as well, and he appeared with various girlfriends from time to time. There was one he seemed really keen on, but one Saturday afternoon, he turned up on his own and came in sobbing.

"Whatever's the matter?" we asked.

Apparently, this girlfriend didn't want to see him anymore. "And you know what she liked the best about me?" he asked. "My hair!"

At this time, he had long hair tied back in a ponytail and was very proud of his locks. "Well, she can have it!" he shouted. He promptly grabbed a pair of scissors and hacked it off, there and then, and stuffed it all in an envelope. Then he stomped off to post it through her letterbox!

When he came back and saw what a fright he looked, with his remaining clumps of chopped hair and an elastic band still dangling from some missed strands, he dashed round to a mate's house and got him to shave the rest of it off. He looked quite handsome afterwards!

When Eliza was about 2 years old, Tom and Melissa moved away to Leicester. Tom had some family there and apparently there were some good job prospects and housing opportunities. We were sad to see them go and would miss them, but at the same time, we were happy to see them trying to improve their lot.

Shortly after Tom and Melissa had left Crayford, Jim made a surprising move. He started coming to the Bible meetings with the children and me. He seemed to be behaving better as well. It wasn't long before he got himself back in good standing and was welcomed back into the group. We had some lovely dinner invitations, and everybody said how happy I must be now. I said yes, but really, it was so terribly difficult because too much damage had been done. I just couldn't feel as happy as I thought I should. I had got to the point where I just couldn't stand him even being near me.

A lovely disabled couple from our group realised we were struggling financially and gave Jim some painting and decorating work in their home. This lasted for several weeks, and they paid him well for it. Some days he would come back from there with a huge joint of meat he said they'd given him. I said I would thank them for it too, but Jim said not to as they'd be embarrassed. So I didn't. But it did make me wonder if he'd just helped himself as I knew this couple always had a hugely stocked cupboard and fridge freezer. And it was definitely the sort of thing that Jim would have done in the past. I wasn't totally convinced that he'd changed his ways but was frightened to check.

Sometimes at our Bible meetings, we'd be chatting to our friends, and Jim, ever the joker, would make a disparaging remark or joke about me. It was hurtful. Privately, those friends would say to me not to worry too much about it because, they said, if he keeps coming, he'll eventually realise what's appropriate and what's not.

Then he didn't come with us for some time. He claimed to be ill and lay on the settee under the *Mr Men* blanket. Some of our friends sent him cheery get-well cards, though I doubted he was really physically ill.

Then the bad treatment resumed. The obsession with me wetting myself, although there had been a bit of a break from it during his good efforts, all restarted. Sometimes he wanted me to do it beside the bed while he masturbated. I couldn't bear this. It seemed wrong on so many levels, and I hated having to scrub that area of the carpet practically every morning. I tried my hardest to protest but was so afraid of his bullying tactics that I felt I had to go along with it, to save injury of some sort in retaliation as I'd so often experienced previously. I'd had enough hospital visits to last a lifetime and tried my hardest to avoid any more.

This bedtime problem wasn't instead of our nightly walks. It was *as well as*. I couldn't understand how someone could be so sex mad after twenty years of marriage. I had well and truly gone off it completely. Sometimes, when we were in bed and he was on top of me, I would imagine that I had a knife hidden under the mattress and I could just pull it out and plunge it into his back. What a relief that would be. I often had that thought but never acted on it.

There was another alternative. When he wasn't around, I would gather up all the tablets I could find, including paracetamol, aspirins, Distalgesic, and more. Jim always had a huge stash of medication. Then I would line them up on the windowsill and consider taking them all. I'd tried it several times years earlier and it had never worked, but it didn't stop me from considering it again.

But then I would think of the little ones. I thought I should make an arrangement with my older daughter to take them on. Speak to her. Have something in writing. But then it all became so complicated and confusing, and after I'd taken maybe just two or three of the tablets, I'd scoop the rest of them up and put them back in their bottles. Then I'd have a good cry for the worthless, nothing person I was.

Meanwhile, I was still putting on a smiling face and going to the Bible meetings. There some of them would ask after my "dear husband". Now and again, he would still come with us, but more often than not, he would be at home under his favourite blanket.

The night-time walks and bedroom problems continued. It made no difference how "ill" he had been through the day. He would get a new lease of life as the evening wore on.

One night I was standing beside the bed, where he expected me to wet myself. He had plied me with coffee and juice throughout the evening, to make sure that I had a full bladder, and he wouldn't allow me to go to the bathroom through the evening either. But as I stood there, something caught my eye. There were two bare wires poking out from under the bed. I couldn't see what they were attached to, but it frightened me. I just could not do as he commanded. There was no way I would risk standing there in my bare feet and wet myself with bare wires there. When I refused to go, he sent me to get him a drink of water and to be quick, with no toilet stop on the way. I wanted to but didn't dare and ran back upstairs with his water that he put on his bedside cupboard. He kept mauling me and kissing me from his bed and tried to pull me really close, but I just was not going to step on those wires. Then he "accidentally" knocked his water to the floor, but instinct made me jump back quickly. Eventually, he allowed me in the bed, and when I could hear him breathing deeply, I knew he was asleep. So I crept down to the bathroom to relieve myself at last.

Sometimes when we went up to bed, the wires were there, and sometimes they weren't. They were never very obvious. I had no idea exactly what they were or where they went, and I never let on to him that I knew about them, but I was very, very frightened.

One day when Jim was out, I thought I would investigate the wire business and went on the hunt for them. I discovered a box in the cupboard above his wardrobe where I could actually see the wires sticking up. I was just going to reach up to fetch the box down, but I bottled out. What if Jim came back at that moment and saw me? Or would he be able to tell later that I'd found it and maybe not put it back exactly as he'd left it? Also, I was afraid of what I'd find there. But now that I knew where he kept it, every time I went to bed, I'd check if the box was still in the cupboard, and if it wasn't, I knew that I had to be especially careful.

Other tactics of his continued, including his huge hands around my throat during sex. I always managed to fight for breath. Other times it was a pillow over my face where, again, I'd try my hardest to fight it off. It was just all so unbearable. The days were spent putting up with his bad temper, maybe having dinners thrown up the wall or glasses smashed or thrown at me and just dreading what was to come at the end of the day. The evenings were worse, not being allowed to leave the living room except to put the little ones to bed or to make tea, while Jim would guard the bathroom to make sure I didn't go in. Then the very worst was when the children were in bed and asleep. Mark was the only older one at home now, and through the night, there were times when I'd run into his bedroom for safety when I thought Jim was trying to kill me. I don't think Mark ever woke up when I went in, but I felt sure that Jim wouldn't attack me there.

The money situation was dire too, never knowing where the next meal would come from and scouring the back alleyways regularly for dropped coins. So I went back down to the agency and got some more work. I wasn't confident enough to get back into the better-paid office work of my younger days and was sent to a factory called Egertons in St Mary's Cray. The agency sent a van to pick us up in town and brought us back at the end of the day.

Sixteen-year-old Carla, mentioned in the first chapter, and I were the only girls in the van, so we palled up. The rest were young lads, and my Mark even got a job there too for a while. On the way home from work, two of the lads always fell asleep, and we girls had great fun putting our make-up on their faces!

At the factory, I met Marty, and as outlined again in the first chapter, we seemed to really hit it off. He was a conscientious worker. One day a week he went to college, and two evenings a week he taught judo. He wasn't a typical factory lad and took a lot of stick from the others there. But somehow, we gelled. I think on reflection he was looking for a mother figure, having been brought up by his gran. And I—well, I was just needy. During my marriage, I'd not been allowed interaction with other men of my age, but having teenage sons, I found it easy with young men. I don't believe any flirting went on between us, just a comfortable companionship. We might do a bit of teasing throughout the day and we'd have our lunch together and chat. A couple of times, we went out to the car park and I rode his bike around. Just a little harmless fun, and I enjoyed it. After all, there wasn't much to enjoy at home. Another lunchtime we looked at some motor racing photos together.

Much as I enjoyed his friendship, I never told Marty anything about my private life, though he did confide a lot in me about his past, and he'd experienced a lot of sadness. I wished that I could heal him, but if just listening helped, that was all I could do, and I was happy to do it. He was a very sensitive young man, which I found out early on over the poem as detailed in the first chapter. Carla and I'd had so much fun with the poem, and we were quite shocked by his reaction. She said she couldn't be bothered with him after that, but I wanted to understand his upset so I did get to know him and care about him.

Things at home changed. Melissa and Tom offered Mark to go and live with them in Leicester, where good jobs were plentiful. I had known it was only a matter of time before he moved out, but it came sooner than I had expected. I would miss him, and I would no longer have a "safe" bedroom to run to. And that frightened me.

I carried on working at the factory. In fact, I had left the agency and worked directly for Egertons, which made the job more secure. But then Marty suddenly started to avoid me, and I had no idea why. Apparently, he'd asked to be moved elsewhere in the factory, so I would only see him occasionally when he walked through our area. At lunchtimes, there was no sign of him either. I pretended that I wasn't bothered, but really I was. After asking Carla one or two questions, I discovered that there had been a lot of gossip going on about the two of us. Marty had been teased about his "older woman", and I had been totally oblivious to it. It had all been so innocent as well.

But I went home and thought about it. I realised that I cared so much about that boy. I loved him, and I missed him so much. He'd brought a little bit of brightness to my sad days, and that had now gone. I even started to fantasise about him. Never in a sexual way. Those desires had well and truly been killed. But I'd imagine just watching television with him, snuggled against him on the settee. Maybe crying on his shoulder, not sure what about, but he would be so kind and caring to me.

How I hated myself for having these thoughts and daydreams. I was married, and marriage was a sacred arrangement. I shouldn't be craving care and kindness elsewhere. And Marty was only 21, the same age as my Melissa. It was just all so wrong and messed up.

CHAPTER 30

Countdown

I HAD A LOT OF thinking to do. I was so desperately unhappy. I still felt that I wanted to take my own life, and if I didn't, I thought that in the end Jim would. The older children were off making their own lives in the world now, but I still had the three younger ones to think of.

At work, Marty continued to ignore me on the few times he passed by, and I continued to pretend I wasn't bothered. But there was another nice, young lad there who had made friends with my Mark when he had worked with us. One day this lad said to me, "You must come and meet my mum. She's smashing. You'll love her." They only lived ten minutes away from the factory, and he told me that she belonged to the same Bible group as me, but of course her local one. He said he would take me one lunchtime. I asked him if he was sure, after all the gossip from my friendship with Marty. He said he didn't care, so one lunchtime we walked up together.

I *did* love her, and she *was* smashing, and Vee and I became good friends. I'd go up a couple of times a week with my sandwiches, and she would make me some coffee.

Somehow, after several lunchtime visits, I started to confide in her about the awful treatment I was getting at home. I don't know what prompted me to tell her, as I'd never told anyone before, but maybe because it was all coming to a head, and I felt safe telling her because she was someone that Jim didn't know or know of even.

One day she said to me, "You shouldn't have to go through all this."

"I don't have a choice," I replied.

"Of *course* you do," she said. "Think about it."

Did I have a choice? I thought about this so much after that conversation and prayed about my situation in earnest. One day I was walking into town by myself, trying to stop tears rolling down my cheeks, and praying as I went. I even said in my prayer, "I wish, God, that you could hold my hand." Then I stopped and laughed! What a stupid thing to say to God almighty!

The next day at our Bible group, we read the most amazing verse from the book of Isaiah 41:13 (King James Version). It said, "For I the LORD thy God will hold thy right hand, saying unto thee, Fear not; I will help thee." I couldn't believe what I was seeing. God had answered my prayer! I'd never abandoned him, and I could see that he hadn't abandoned me either. This gave me the extra strength to keep going, with no more suicidal thoughts, and to think and plan seriously what I was going to do about my situation.

So yes, I made a six-week plan, starting then in December and taking me to the nineteenth of January, and on that day, I would take the children and just go. Where? Well, I didn't know yet, but I had got six weeks to organise something.

I never told a soul. Not my children, not my mother or sister, not the Bible group leaders, and not even my friend Vee. I had to do this for myself.

The plan was as follows:

- to remain calm for the six weeks
- to decide what to take with me
- to phone Women's Aid
- to find out where I should go when I leave
- to give notice to my job
- just before I leave to let the Bible group leaders know what I'm doing and why
- to look for birth certificates and other important papers
- countdown chart

Of course, my plan and countdown chart weren't written down, but they were very clear in my head.

For the first two weeks, I didn't do anything from the list except to mull it over in my mind. This would be the biggest and hardest thing I would ever do, so I had to be really careful, and I had to do it properly. Although I wasn't sure what "properly" actually was.

After two weeks, I telephoned the Women's Aid organisation and asked about accommodation in the refuges and safe houses. They told me they could put me in a room in the Lewisham refuge that day. I said I wasn't ready to go yet and was just checking. But they told me I would have to telephone them on the day that I left, as what was available one day wasn't necessarily available the next. So that was one thing from my list dealt with, as much as it could be for the moment.

Next, I made sure that our birth certificates and other necessary paperwork were all together.

Then I *did* tell someone. I told my workmate Sue, who picked me up in Crayford and drove me to work and back each day. Again, she was someone Jim didn't know, and she lived in a village the other side of Crayford, so they weren't likely to cross paths any time either. This was another part of my plan. I wanted to stash a few things with her, if she was agreeable, and to collect them once I had left and settled somewhere. I didn't go into any detail but just said I was leaving my husband because of cruelty. She was sad for me and agreed to my request. She also promised not to say anything to anyone at work.

I think the first bag I left with her had a few items of underwear for the children and me. Only a couple of changes, as I had to have enough at home for the time being. I also gave her a black bin bag to put everything in as and when I gave it to her. Another time I took a favourite dress to go into the black bag. I didn't take things every day as I didn't want Jim to be suspicious of the extra carrier bags I was taking to work.

I did a lot of praying through the six weeks. I really wanted to know that I was doing the right thing. I'd been brought up to believe that the only grounds for divorce according to Bible scripture was adultery. I knew what I had seen but had no idea how I could prove that. Then to my surprise, we had a magazine released for our Bible group about marriage and the Bible's view. In the magazine, it detailed three or four distinct reasons where it would be reasonable to leave a spouse, and I ticked all the boxes. One was for wilful non-support materially. Well, he never had. And another one was if you felt that your life was in danger. Definitely yes to that one too. Another prayer answered. It was as if God was saying to me, "Yes, Helen, go."

When it came to the Christmas holidays, we went as a family to stay for a few days with Hannah and her husband, and my mother too as she was living there. It was lovely to see them but quite a strain to pretend that everything was fine. I must have pulled it off though as they never asked any awkward questions. It was coming up to their silver wedding anniversary in March, and we were invited to the party they were planning. I had never known them to have a party, and the idea really appealed to me. We said we would love to come, while at the same time, I knew that I wouldn't be going. I just couldn't tell them yet.

After the holidays, I went back to work, and gave a couple more bags to Sue. One had a bottle of Bailey's Irish Cream that my friend Janet had given me a while back, in thanks for looking after Chrissie. I wrapped it in a towel for protection, and of course, the towel would be useful.

Time was going by and the countdown chart in my head was well over halfway now. My nerves were really bad, but I hid it as best as I could, and Jim didn't seem to notice. Probably because he was too busy being "poorly" under the *Mr Men* blanket. I found it very difficult to eat anything, and at work, I only had a yoghurt.

With just over a week to go, I went in to see my supervisors at the factory and gave in my notice. My voice was shaky, and they asked if I was OK. So I told them my plan to leave, without divulging too much detail. They got the gist of it and were very kind, putting me to work on my own at an easy job for my last week there. They had me near their office, in case I wanted to see them, and near to the ladies, in case I needed to go and have a little cry, which I did a few times.

On the Monday of that last week, through the evening, I noticed Brad on his front doorstep. His children were in bed, no doubt, and Sam was working nights that week. On impulse, I went across to him and said, "Can you give me a hug please?" Rightly or wrongly, I couldn't think of anything I needed more at that moment.

He asked if I was OK, and I said, "Yes, but I just really need a hug."

And he did. It felt so warm and comforting. There was nothing sexual in it, and I felt safe and unafraid, particularly knowing it wasn't going to lead to anything unpleasant. That good feeling kept me going that night.

Tuesday and Wednesday evenings, I asked him again for a hug, and again, he did. No questions asked.

Thursday evening was a Bible meeting night. Jim said he wasn't coming, so I went with the three children. I knew this would be my last meeting there, and I needed to let the group leaders know what I was going to do and why, so I asked one of them if I could speak to him afterwards. I was so tense and worried about what I would say that I don't think I heard a word of what was said during the actual meeting.

After it had finished, it was a long time before I got to speak to the leader as there was a lot going on that evening. We'd all been given some identity cards, and the leaders were signing them, so I had to wait until after that was done. I was very worried about getting home later than usual, because Jim would interrogate me if he thought I was ever late back. He would ask, "Have you been talking about me?" and I would say no. But I couldn't say no this time if he asked because it would be a lie.

After almost everyone had left, two of the leaders took me to a quiet corner to talk while one of the wives kept the children occupied. Then it all came pouring out. I have no idea what I said. I was in such a state, and I'm sure there were lots of tears too. They called another of the leaders to come and listen, as it was obviously very serious. I do remember saying, "I haven't come to ask your advice. I've come to tell you what I'm doing."

None of them tried to change my mind, and it was agreed that on Saturday, once I'd got to wherever I was going to be, I would phone one of them, then they would go and see Jim. After the discussion, one of them gave the children and me a lift home.

I was shaking when I went in the front door as we were later than ever this evening and I dreaded what was to come. But Jim was glued to something on the television, and as we came into the living room, he just glanced up, put his finger to his lips, and said, "Shhh. I'm watching this."

I am a Real Person

I put the children to bed, and then I crept out and knocked on Brad's door for my hug. That kept me going until the morning.

Friday—the last day on my countdown chart. I knew this wouldn't be an easy day. I put the birth certificates and some other paperwork in a carrier bag, along with a few other last-minute bits and pieces. I was just about to leave for work with it when Jim called down from the bedroom, "I'll give you a lift down." He had the use of his ex-boss's van and was hoping to buy it from him.

This was worrying. I had this extra carrier bag, and I was certain that he'd ask what was in it. But most surprisingly, he didn't ask.

He dropped me off in town for me to pick up my lift with Sue.

My last day at work, and still nobody knew I was leaving except for my supervisors and Sue. I don't think I did much work that day, and I couldn't eat my lunchtime yoghurt. My supervisors were very kind and wished me all the best for the future. I still didn't want to tell anyone else there that I was leaving that day because I couldn't face any fuss.

I clocked out as usual at the end of the day and went to walk out of the door with Sue. Then I saw Jim waving at me from the van on the road outside. I hadn't expected that! I was so glad I hadn't told anyone else, and Sue just whispered, "Good luck." I climbed in, and Jim shouted loudly "Anyone want a lift? Crayford or near!" And one of my workmates ran over. "Yes, please, but Sidcup if you can." Sidcup was more or less on the way, so she jumped in as well. When we dropped her off, she offered us in for a cup of tea as a thank you, and Jim said, "Yes, please."

How glad I was that she had no idea of the situation.

I couldn't wait to get back home and for the day to be over, so I was relieved when we left after half an hour. "See you on Monday, Helen," she called as we left.

But then before we were out of Sidcup, Jim spotted someone we knew from back when we had lived in the area, so he stopped to chat. That seemed to take forever, and we got invited to go over the following weekend. Well, that wouldn't be happening. Not for me anyway.

It was a relief to get home and do the normal late afternoon and evening things, like having dinner and putting the children to bed, all done on autopilot. Jim told me that he had a day's work with Jonno the next day. I was glad because that would make it easy for us to leave after he'd gone off with Jonno.

Jim dozed off on the settee through the evening, and I crept out and over to Brad for my hug. "This is the last one," I said.

He still didn't ask any questions, though I did wonder if he had guessed, as although he had never commented on it, I'm sure he was aware of some of Jim's treatment of me. That last hug carried me through to the next day.

For all my planning and my countdown chart, I had no idea how the next day would pan out. But tomorrow was the day, and I just knew that I had to go.

CHAPTER 31

Escape!

19 JANUARY SATURDAY

Today was the day. The countdown chart was done, and if anything had been left off from the plan, well, it was too late now. Today was the day, and I had to keep a clear head.

Normally I dreaded Jonno coming, but today I couldn't wait for him to arrive so that they would both go off to work and leave it clear for me to go.

But when Jonno arrived, Jim said, "I think we'll take Micah to work with us today."

He had never taken Micah to work with him before, so I was most surprised by this and it threw me completely. I had to think of something quick because I couldn't leave without my boy. He was only 11, and there was no way I would abandon him. I had a very quick brainwave and said I was taking the children to a friend's for a haircut. This was someone I used to work with and she'd cut our hair before at her home.

"I can take Micah to the barbers with me when I go," he replied.

Nooo. More quick thinking was required.

"Well, I'd like him to come because she's got something in her garage for him," I said. Now this was a lie, and I felt really bad about it. But I just didn't know what else to say.

Fortunately, he agreed to this and said he would drop us off at my friend's house, and he took us all along with Jonno in the van. It was just the other side of the town. We could have walked there. But when I got out of the van, he said, "How long will you be? And I'll pick you up."

"About an hour," I replied.

He said, "See you later," and drove off. I guessed he was coming back for us so that he could still take Micah to work with him.

My friend let us in and I asked if she could cut Amanda's hair. She put the kettle on for a drink and went to get her scissors. Then I panicked. I hadn't expected Jim to come back for us and said, "Sorry, my plans have changed and I need to go. Can I use your phone to call a cab please?" And that's what I did.

Within a few minutes, the cab arrived. I apologised to my friend for our very brief visit. But I had great difficulty getting Micah into the car. He kept saying, "But dad's coming back for us."

"Just get in. I know what I'm doing," I said to him.

I asked the cab driver to take us to St Mary's Cray. I knew I had to get out of the immediate area. We were heading to Vee's. It wasn't part of the plan, but that had all gone out of my head with the events of the morning.

I asked the driver to drop us off at the end of an alleyway that led to Vee's house rather than to drop us at her door. This was because I thought that Jim might be able to track where we were from the cab company. The end of the alley was a decoy.

Vee was very surprised to see the children and me. She'd not met them before and welcomed us in, whereupon I burst into tears.

Hugs, coffee, and a call to her local group leaders, and I managed to pull myself together in time for two of them to come and talk to me and give what help they could. Calling Women's Aid as planned was not an option as no one was managing the phones at the weekends back then.

I hugged and thanked my dear friend. Then Dave, one of the leaders, drove us to Orpington Police Station, where he told them of my plight. They asked me some more questions, then they organised for the three children and me to go into a room in a shared house in Gravesend for the weekend. On the Monday, I was to go to the Council offices in Bexleyheath and present myself as homeless and no doubt tell the whole sorry story all over again.

Dave was very kind. He gave the children an apple each and drove us to the Gravesend address, before leaving us to go back to his own family. I really did appreciate all his time and help.

Our room was in the basement, so we could look through the window at passer-by's legs and feet. It was a very basic room with three single beds, a sink, and an electric radiator. There was a shared kitchen and bathroom, and all the other rooms had little families living on a temporary basis.

Before someone took us to our room, we went into a shared common room that was by the front door. I noticed a couple of packs of playing cards on the coffee table so I encouraged the children to play. It kept them occupied. I think one or two of the other residents sitting in the room were quite surprised to see the children playing rummy, especially with Amanda being just 5 years old. Their older siblings had taught them several card games and some tricks even when they were all really little.

While they were playing cards, I found a payphone in the hallway and telephoned the Crayford group leader as promised. I told him where we were for the weekend, and he said that two of them would go round and see Jim and tell him that I wasn't coming back. He asked if we were OK and said to ring him again after the Council had put us somewhere. I said we were all OK, although really, I was just numb. No amount of planning could have prepared me as I'd had no idea what to expect when I left Crayford.

All I'd brought with me in my bag was my purse, family allowance book, and a hairbrush, so I was not particularly prepared for our weekend there. We went out and found a fish and chip shop and I bought some chips to eat back in our room. My biggest problem was Micah. He was angry one minute and upset the next. He'd never been an angry child, and I found this very difficult. He really wasn't coping with the situation. He kept saying I had lied to his dad and he wanted to go home. I just said that I'd had to but didn't want to explain as I didn't think he'd seen or known of the bigger problems. I really wanted to protect the younger ones from it.

But he still kept shouting at me and started to even hit me. Then he ran out of the room and the house and said he was going home. I tried to pull him back in, but he kept lashing out at me and screaming. Then he hurled his chips into the gutter and declared that he didn't want to be anywhere near me and he was going home. He knew the way. We'd passed the station and he was a pretty clued-up 11-year-old so I knew that he could get back.

I realised that I had lost this battle. Rather than have him run off and get into trouble for jumping the train, I gave him some money for his fare back to his dad. I tried to hug him and tell him I loved him before he went, but he shouted me down and wouldn't let me get near him. It was heartbreaking.

Back in our room, I'd lost my appetite for my chips, but James and Amanda enjoyed theirs. After they had finished, I tucked them up in their beds wearing only their vests, and I washed the rest of their underwear and mine in the little sink, and then hung it all over the radiator to dry for the morning.

I didn't think that I would sleep because I was so upset about Micah, but I must have been exhausted—mentally at least. I actually slept really well that night.

But I had quite a shock first thing in the morning. Someone was repeatedly banging on the front door, and I could see Jim's white van parked outside our window. Thankfully, nobody opened the door. I believe it was their policy not to open the door to anyone unexpected. I hadn't reckoned on Micah bringing his dad back to the house. Of course, Micah knew which was our room, and when they gave up knocking, they stood on the pavement outside, shouting down to us. I kept the curtains closed and could just see them through a small gap. I thought they were going to stay there all day so I had no intention of leaving the house at all. There were a few bits in the kitchen, which Janey, one of the other residents, had said I could use for a meal. She also had said that she would come on the bus with us to Bexleyheath on Monday.

Eventually, Jim and Micah must have left. Then I must have made the children some lunch and dinner, and I remember that I washed our underwear in the sink again ready for Monday, but everything else that day is now a blur. I was just numb.

Monday morning, we got up and ready to get the bus with Janey to Bexleyheath for the Council offices. After her children had left for school, Janey knocked on our door and we set off together. I was glad of her company as the bus would go through Crayford on its way, and there was no way to avoid that.

We parted company in Bexleyheath and wished each other all the best. She was waiting to be housed along with her husband and children. And me? I didn't know quite what to expect.

Inside the offices, I was shown straight into a private room and the door was locked. It wasn't really private at all though. The walls were made of toughened glass, I think, so we could see out into the foyer and anyone could see in if they chose to.

I was sorry not to be able to see Jane Templer, our original housing officer who had always looked out for us. She had sadly passed away a year or two earlier. Another lady came out to speak to us. She already knew of our situation, but we still had to go through lots of paperwork. While we were in there with her, I suddenly became aware of shouting and screaming outside our room. It was Jim with Micah, shouting, swearing, and carrying on and thumping the glass between us. Some Council staff quickly appeared and tried to calm him down, and then the crying and weeping started. Both of them at once.

I kept mine and the children's backs to what was going on in the foyer. I was very frightened and hugged Amanda onto my lap, as much for my benefit as hers. I was terrified that he would get to us and make us go back home. But worse than that, it was awful knowing that my Micah was out there too. I'd forgotten that he would've heard me being told to go to the Council on Monday morning and would report that back to his dad. I so badly wanted him with me that it almost made me run out and grab him. Quite quickly, several police officers arrived and took control of the situation. They eventually managed to usher Jim and Micah out of the Council offices.

I was told we were going to a women's refuge in Canterbury and was given the address and a travel warrant for the train journey. I was even given enough money for a cab at the other end. She told me the refuge would be expecting me. Then we were led out through a passageway and through the back of the offices to a waiting cab that would take us to Bromley train station.

The driver was told to keep an eye out for Jim's white van in case he was still about and tried to follow us, and we were told to lie down on the back seat of the cab so that we wouldn't be seen if he was.

So in that way, James, Amanda, and I left the area completely, ready for our new life.

CHAPTER 32

The Refuge

OUR JOURNEY WENT WITHOUT HICCUP, and we arrived at the refuge at about three o'clock that Monday. As the doors shut behind us, I gave a huge sigh of relief.

I was welcomed by two social workers who took me straight into their office. I found out later their names were Ellie and Jan. They were a great team. Ellie was the tough one and Jan the soft, gentle worker. They were due to finish there at three o'clock so they introduced me to a couple of the girls before promising to see me back in the office the next morning.

One of the girls, Marie, took us upstairs and showed us the room that was to be our home for the next few months to a year. It was a large bedroom facing the main road, with a single bed and a set of bunks that Marie had made up earlier with fresh bedding for us. It had a large wardrobe, two chests of drawers, a fold-up table, and three dining chairs. Nothing posh, nothing matching, and probably all as old as Noah's ark!

I flung myself on the single bed with another big sigh. I felt safe at last, and for a brief moment, it seemed as if Marie were a heaven-sent mother looking down and smiling at me—despite the fact that she was probably a good fifteen years younger than me and about six inches shorter! Then the children tried the bunks. It was almost a disaster. They were so wobbly as to be unsafe to sleep on. It didn't spoil our good feeling though. Marie rounded up two or three other women, and between them, they dismantled the bunks and rearranged the room to fit the beds in separately. I think we all laughed more in that half hour than I had done in twenty years of marriage!

After the bedroom was sorted out, Marie showed us her room across the landing, where she had lived with her three children for over a year already. Then she took us on a tour of the rest of the house.

There were several toilets, bathrooms, and shower rooms as well as a huge kitchen with several cookers and sinks, rows of cupboards, and a couple of large fridges for communal use. Marie explained that in general, we catered for our own families. There was a dining room next to the kitchen with a massive table, an odd assortment of dining chairs, and a couple of high chairs, all looking as if they could do with a good scrub with bleach and disinfectant. (Marie pointed out that some families preferred to eat in their bedrooms.)

There was also a laundry room with two washing machines, a dryer, and several clothes airers. I was to discover later on that some children, too small yet for school, thought it great fun to fiddle with the washing machine knobs, and I often heard the girls grumbling about colours running in the wash and jumpers shrinking. In the end, we managed to have a lock fitted onto the laundry room door, though more times than once a toddler was caught scrambling up on a chair to get to it, and another time, somebody's little girl actually got locked in there. We held a search for about two hours before we eventually found her.

After our tour of the house, Marie took us to the large, communal lounge that consisted of two or three old settees, several battered armchairs, and a television, video player, and radio positioned supposedly out of the children's reach. Off the side of the lounge was a nursery room where the toddlers could be supervised in the mornings. Several women were sitting around chatting and smoking. I wrinkled my nose at the smell and winced at the loudness of the television, which nobody seemed to be watching.

"You don't have to sit down here," said Marie. "When we don't feel like company, we just stay up in our rooms."

I looked around at the women, and Marie introduced me to them and their children. I thought I would never remember which children belonged to who! I recognised one of the women there, Dawn. The social workers had introduced me to her earlier. She had two small boys who were obviously quite a handful. Then Dawn went off down the road and brought back fish and chips for her boys and some for my children and me. I was very grateful. I hadn't even thought about a meal for the evening. Over the months we were there, I discovered that Dawn was a lot like me. We gradually became good friends.

I slept really well that night. In fact, not just that night but throughout my entire stay there. It felt as if the house were putting its arms around my children and me to keep us safe.

In the refuge, there were enough rooms for twelve women and their children. We were a mixed crowd. Some very rough and ready, and just one or two quite upper class. We also had a gipsy girl whose life was in danger from an entire family at that time, and there was another young girl of 18 who'd been there with her mother and little brother. Her name was Selina. Her mother had taken her son and gone back to her husband, but Selina had vowed never to go back as she was so afraid of her stepfather. So she was allowed to stay on at the house.

In fact, within a few weeks, Selina's mother had to run away again, but because her husband had wheedled the telephone number of the Canterbury refuge out of her, it was not safe for her to return. The social workers made arrangements for her to stay at a refuge elsewhere and arranged for Selina to join her a few days later.

I'd never met her mother but joined in the sad farewells to Selina. We'd all become quite fond of her, and the children adored her. She'd made a good babysitter, having no job or other obligations to restrict her.

We never heard any more from Selina or her mother, but that certainly wasn't the end of it. Selina's stepfather, David, refused to believe that his family had not returned to our refuge, and he used to phone up three or four times a day, sometimes quite late at night, asking for them. Sometimes he was crying, and sometimes he was shouting and screaming abuse. We all took turns in answering the phone to him. Ellie and Jan told us to hang up straight away when he called, but some of the girls were so full up with anger and hatred because of the treatment they'd received from their own partners that they were only too pleased to talk to David and take out all their feelings on him. Other girls were just so desperate for male company, though still too frightened to feel safe with a man, that they actually enjoyed talking to

David, almost "chatting him up"—though certainly not in the hearing of our social workers. Then there were those who tried to calm him down by reasoning with him. But David was not a man to reason with. It took several months before he gave up phoning us.

We had to look after our own bedrooms, but there was a rota for the rest of the house. Each week we were assigned a different job—maybe keeping the lounge clean and tidy or the kitchen, toilets, stairs, and so on. We were supposed to do our jobs as we would in our own homes. Some girls never did their jobs, others only half-heartedly, and a few girls were very conscientious, so it was just as well that we changed jobs each week. Sometimes Ellie would come into the lounge and shout at us all about the state of the house. Then we'd have an absolute blitz washing windows, scrubbing walls, and clearing cigarette butts, toast, and sweet wrappers from underneath the settee cushions. There was always a queue for the bathroom afterwards.

In the mornings, the children gathered in the hallway, ready to be taken to the local primary school. We'd take turns to escort them, usually between two or four of us at a time, depending on the number of children going. The school wasn't very far away and they were very accommodating to our children, knowing that it was just a temporary arrangement until we moved on.

Every Friday morning, we had a house meeting where everyone was expected to come and air their views, problems, and grievances. Once or twice the meetings became heated, usually with conflicts over each other's children, but mostly these meetings were pleasant and friendly occasions with Ellie or Jan keeping the peace.

Also, on Fridays Janice came. She was the refuge counsellor. Not everyone saw her. Some didn't need to, and some didn't want to. Ellie and Jan had arranged for me to see her weekly as I was in such a state when I arrived.

Janice was lovely. She didn't say a lot, just enough to draw me out, though it took several weeks before I started to talk. She did tell me, a good two years later, that she had been so concerned about me at first that she was going to refer me to a psychiatrist, until she finally got through to me.

I AM A REAL PERSON

When I left the refuge and moved to a little house in Swalecliffe, I used to go back to the refuge every Friday to continue my counselling. I saw Janice regularly for two years until she moved away from the area. I will always be grateful to her for her patience with me as I know I used to ramble on to her sometimes.

I will always be grateful to Ellie and Jan as well. The morning after our arrival at the refuge, I went into their office, and they immediately made me feel at ease. They arranged an appointment for me to go to the local social security offices about a payment that same day. They got me registered with a doctor and arranged for the children to start school the following week. They even contacted the local Bible group leaders for me.

They also arranged for us to visit the local solicitors' office if and when it became necessary, very often accompanying us on our many trips to court. Then when we returned, we'd be straight in the office pouring it all out, maybe having a good cry or a shout to relieve our pent-up feelings. Sometimes we carried on in quite an unreasonable way to our very patient social workers. But they always listened and supported us.

In the school holidays, they arranged local trips for us using a hired minibus. We went to Dreamland funfair in Margate more than once and to Brambles Wildlife Park in Herne Bay. Occasionally they paid for our children to go to the cinema.

In general, we all got on very well despite our differences. We were like a large family with everyone an individual. Occasionally one or two of the women would fall out with each other, but just like family, it didn't usually last long. Only on a few occasions did Ellie and Jan have to intervene.

The children had a great time in the refuge. With so many children, they always had someone to play with. There was a nursery in the mornings for the little ones, and when the big ones had school holidays, they went into the nursery as well to help and join in the fun.

There was a big, high-walled garden at the back of the house with swings, a slide, and a climbing frame. In the summer, we used to fill a plastic paddling pool up with water for them. The children all called it the park. We did have a few minor accidents in the garden with one or two children needing stitches, and my own son broke his arm doing something stupid on a baby's tricycle.

We became good friends with the girl in the next bedroom. She arrived at the refuge three weeks after me, and I remember helping her in with all her luggage. She certainly came prepared. She had suitcases full of clothes and belongings, a very heavy television, and a video player. It took several trips up and downstairs to get it all to her room. I'd only brought a purse and hairbrush when I'd arrived!

She looked around suspiciously at us all, not just that day but for several weeks after. That was Frances, who turned out to be quite a character once she came to terms with herself and her situation.

She had a little girl the same age as Amanda, and she had twins, John and Gemma. They were sweet, little, tiny toddlers who held hands and did everything together. They got into all sorts of scrapes and had a fondness for sharing out all of Frances's biscuits amongst the other children. When the biscuits ran out, they went back to their room and found anything else they could share. What food was left they would tip out and trample into their bedroom floor along with soap powder, milk, and whatever else they could reach. Nothing could be hidden out of their way. They were an excellent team and wonderful climbers. They spoke their own language known only to them. We all loved the twins, but poor Frances repeatedly tore her hair out over them.

Frances was three months' pregnant when she moved into the house. No one believed her. That was because another girl there was heavily pregnant at the time, and it seemed as if anything anyone had done, Frances had done before. We found out later it was true. Frances had done everything!

When the time came for Frances to have her baby, there was great excitement in the house. She was whisked off to the hospital and the rest of us rallied round and looked after the children for her. We got her room ready and put together the beautiful swinging cot that she'd bought from one of the girls and made it up ready for the baby. We had big celebrations when she returned from hospital with her new little boy.

We also had celebrations whenever one of us was allocated our new home. A girls-only party of course, with the children all tucked up in bed. Someone would make a cake, and we'd sneak in the beer and cider after Ellie and Jan had gone home. There was laughing, and giggling, and dancing, and a few tears sometimes. When someone moved on, our feelings were very mixed. Happy that they were ready for their new life, sad to be losing them from the house, and sometimes envious. We all wanted our turn to come. The next morning, there was always plenty of clearing up to be done in the lounge, and the social workers knew what we'd been up to.

Another occasion that made for great excitement was when the "sandwich man" came, about once a fortnight. This was a gentleman from the Salvation Army who brought sandwiches, pies, and yoghurts from Marks & Spencer that had reached their sell-by date. We had a real feast on those days, and once again, there was a lot of mess to clear up afterwards.

We were always grateful for bits of furniture donated to the house from time to time, and very often bags of clothing were sent in as well. Rag bags we called them. We must have looked like hungry vultures ripping the bags open, gathering up what we liked, and hurling the rest at anyone within reach. The children had a great time dressing up in what was left and parading around the lounge, office, and nursery. We were actually very grateful for the rag bags when we first arrived and were all kitted out from them until we could buy our own clothes.

A few of the women didn't stay very long and returned to their husbands. They complained that the house was too dirty and smelly, other people's children were dirty and smelly, or they didn't get on with some of the other women. I didn't care how dirty or smelly it was there. I was just so relieved to be somewhere that felt safe, and as Marie had pointed out on that first day, we could always stay in our own rooms.

On Sunday mornings, several of us went down to the local boot fair, and we'd come home with all sorts of treasures. Some girls managed to buy decent working televisions for their bedrooms and other household items, ready for when they moved into their new homes. My own best bargains were a small electric organ for one pound and a portable typewriter for two pounds. We've moved on since our days in the refuge. We originally moved to a very pretty house by the sea in Swalecliffe, but various circumstances caused us to move back to Canterbury, where we are very happy and comfortable.

Marie and her children moved out of the refuge shortly after we moved in. She still lives in Canterbury and is very happy.

Frances and her family moved soon after me to a house in Thanington, just outside Canterbury. She promptly filled her home with various pets, which died and were replaced at regular intervals before any of the children noticed. We used to walk across the countryside to visit each other on sunny afternoons. But now Frances has moved away to Sheffield. We still write to each other, and it seems as if she is really enjoying life and doing everything again.

As for Dawn and her two boys, they moved into a large house not far from us. We saw each other often and would sometimes have a cup of coffee together and reminisce about our days in the refuge, exchange news about our mutual friends, or just chat and keep each other up to date with our own bits of news. Dawn had made a new life for herself. She'd met a lovely man who looked after her and her boys, and they settled down happily as a family. Tragically she developed a blood clot that hit the lungs. Dawn was eight weeks' pregnant when she died in hospital. I won't ever forget my friend.

I also won't forget my time in the refuge. Yes, it was a difficult time, but I was happy there. I had peace of mind and lots of support, and most of all, I felt safe. And I'm sure there are probably hundreds of women all over the country who have shared those feelings. For me, the refuge really did live up to its name.

CHAPTER 33

The Next Chapter

SOME YEARS HAVE GONE BY now, but to go back a bit, yes, I did get my bag of stashed bits and pieces from Sue, my ex-workmate. Someone from the Canterbury Bible group drove to get it for me. The bottle of Bailey's I shared with Frances in my room one evening along with some cream cakes when the children were asleep.

The disabled couple my husband had worked for came to visit me in the refuge and took me out to dinner. My suspicions were right. Jim had stolen those joints of meat.

I've since been reconciled with my son Micah. We've never discussed things in any depth, but we have a closeness and an understanding, and that is enough.

I've also discovered that my younger children were far more aware of the situation than I had always believed them to be.

After my two years of counselling with Janice, I had many more years of counselling, cognitive behavioural therapy, and psychotherapy because I was so messed up, and I was diagnosed with PTSD. None of my counsellors or therapists ever told me what I should do, but through their help, I've learned to understand myself and learned why I allowed myself to be treated so badly for so long.

I have found my voice and know that I am entitled to my opinion and to say no when necessary. I know that I am stronger than all I have been through in my past and have learned to deal with it and move on. My time since the refuge has had its ups and downs, and for a long time, I was ashamed of what I'd been through, but putting it in writing has been the final piece of therapy needed, like fitting in the last piece of a jigsaw puzzle. I also like to think that you, the reader, will know that you're not alone if you're going through something similar and that there is always light at the end of the tunnel.

I've always remembered the words of my Crayford group leaders. "We can't help you if we don't know what's wrong." I've joined the Bible group here, and the leaders have been very kind to me. When I first arrived, the Crayford leaders put them in the picture and explained my situation to them, and I have learned to trust them and talk to them if and when necessary.

Of course, we don't have to tell everybody everything, but I do have a few really close friends who I know I can confide in. I had a wonderful friend called Sonia who'd been through some trauma in the early years of her marriage. Not exactly the same as my problems, but we understood and empathised with each other. Sadly, she died of cancer a couple of years ago. I do miss her.

Linda is still a close friend, as are Janet and Karen, and I'd like to thank them for all the support they've given me over the years. I also want to thank my dear friend Vee, who said the right words at the right time and continues to be a good friend.

Another friend who deserves a mention is Natalie, who has now moved to America, but we laughed and cried together many times when she was here. My sister, Hannah, has been very loving and supportive. When I was living in Swalecliffe and first told her about some of the abuse I'd suffered, she cried her eyes out. I do love my big sister.

I'm sure my scriptural beliefs and my faith in God have helped me through, and trying to adhere to Bible principles has kept me with a good conscience, which is worth so much.

So no, there is no magic wand for life, but now I appreciate every single day, and if I've been out anywhere, I never have to be frightened of coming home anymore. This is just priceless. I now have peace of mind.

I am nobody's puppet, and I am nobody's plaything anymore.

I am, at last, *a real person.*

Lightning Source UK Ltd.
Milton Keynes UK
UKHW012047110321
380188UK00001B/34